# THE
# GIBLIN GUIDE to
# WRITING
# CHILDREN'S BOOKS

*Fourth Edition—Revised and Updated*

## by James Cross Giblin

Writer's Institute
Publications

*Cover Illustration:* Robert Pizzo

*Suggested Reading:* Barbara Stretton

*Copyeditor:* Cheryl de la Guéronnière

*Production and Text Design:* Joanna L. Horvath

*Production:* Marni McNiff

*Production Assistant:* Susan Capone

*Publisher:* Prescott V. Kelly

International Standard Book Number 978-1-889715-54-4
Printed and bound in Canada
10 9 8 7 6 5 4 3 2

1-800-443-6078. www.WritersBookstore.com
email: services@WritersBookstore.com

# Acknowledgments

Special thanks go to the authors and illustrators whose work I have edited, and from whom I have learned so much. Among them are: Carole S. Adler, Ursula Arndt, Edna Barth, Marion Dane Bauer, Jan Brett, Roy Brown, Eve Bunting, Carol and Donald Carrick, Arthur Catherall, Kay Chorao, Eileen Christelow, Michael L. Cooper, Russell Freedman, Dick Gackenbach, Paul Galdone, Mary Downing Hahn, Anna Grossnickle Hines, Mildred Lee, J. J. McCoy, Arnold Madison, Jim Murphy, Lila Perl, Stella Pevsner, Robert Quackenbush, Beatrice Schenk de Regniers, Ron Roy, Gloria Skurzynski, Carla Stevens, Jane Resh Thomas, Margot Tomes, Patricia Willis, Jane Yolen.

Thanks, too, to the editors I've had the privilege of working with: Patricia H. Allen, John Brady, Dorothy Briley, Deborah Brodie, William Brohaugh, Kent L. Brown, Jr., A. S. Burack, Sylvia K. Burack, Marianne Carus, Beatrice Creighton, Barbara Fenton, Lillian N. Gerhardt, Ethel L. Heins, Dianne Hess, Nina Ignatowicz, Elizabeth Isele, Antonia Markiet, Sidney Phillips, Norma Jean Sawicki, Anita Silvey, Dinah Stevenson, Susan M. Tierney, Ann Troy.

Above all, I want to pay tribute to my late mother, Anna Cross Giblin, who was responsible for introducing me to children's books and reading.

*For Sue Alexander, who urged me to write this book, and the late Sylvia K. Burack, who edited and published the original version*

# Author's Note

The first edition of this book appeared in 1990, the same year that I took an early retirement as Editor-in-Chief and Publisher at Clarion Books in order to have more time for my own nonfiction writing. I thought of the book as a sort of summing-up of my children's book editorial career, which had begun 30 years earlier at Criterion Books, and continued at Lothrop, Lee & Shepard, The Seabury Press, and finally at Clarion Books, a separate children's book imprint of Houghton Mifflin Company.

In writing the book, I sought to communicate what I had learned as an editor in ways that would be helpful to writers who were just starting out, as well as established professionals. The first edition had a warm reception, and I was encouraged to revise it and bring it up to date in 1995 and again in 1998. These relatively light revisions weren't difficult for me because I'd kept up with the field after my "retirement" through an ongoing role as a contributing editor at Clarion.

Recently, Prescott Kelly of Writer's Institute Publications invited me to undertake a more extensive revision, one that would bring the book in line with the latest twenty-first century developments in the children's book field. I was happy to accept, hoping that this new edition would inspire and enlighten a whole new generation of aspiring writers for children.

James Cross Giblin
New York City

# Books for Young People
# by James Cross Giblin

*The Rise and Fall of Senator Joe McCarthy*

*Did Fleming Rescue Churchill? A Research Puzzle*

*The Many Rides of Paul Revere*

*The Boy Who Saved Cleveland*

*Good Brother, Bad Brother: The Story of Edwin Booth and John Wilkes Booth*

*The Life and Death of Adolf Hitler*

*The Amazing Life of Benjamin Franklin*

*Secrets of the Sphinx*

*Charles A. Lindbergh: A Human Hero*

*The Mystery of the Mammoth Bones and How It Was Solved*

*Thomas Jefferson: A Picture Book Biography*

*Fireworks, Picnics, and Flags: The Story of the Fourth of July Symbols*

*When Plague Strikes: The Black Death, Smallpox, AIDS*

*The Riddle of the Rosetta Stone: Key to Ancient Egypt*

*George Washington: A Picture Book Biography*

*Chimney Sweeps: Yesterday and Today*

*From Hand to Mouth Or, How We Invented Knives, Forks, Spoons, Chopsticks, and the Table*

*Let There Be Light: A Book About Windows*

*Milk: The Fight for Purity*

*Edith Wilson—The Woman Who Ran the United States*

*Be Seated: A Book About Chairs*

*The Truth About Santa Claus*

*The Truth About Unicorns*

*Walls: Defenses Throughout History*

*The Skyscraper Book*

*The Scarecrow Book* (with Dale Ferguson)

# Table of Contents

 Chapter One

# A Thriving Market

You've decided you want to write a book for children, but you don't know how to get started. Or perhaps you're an established writer who isn't sure just where the children's book field is headed. Whichever the case, you sign up for one of the hundreds of writers' conferences in children's literature that are held throughout the year in virtually every state in the union.

I've spoken as an editor and author at many such conferences, from Los Angeles, California, and Portland, Oregon, to Northampton, Massachusetts, and Sarasota, Florida, but no matter the location, the questions the conferees ask are always the same:

- Why have children's book publishers stopped reading unsolicited manuscripts and how can a writer get around the ban?
- What's the most popular current trend in the children's fiction market?
- How can I tell if there's a market for my nonfiction topic?
- Should I get an illustrator for my picture book story before I submit the manuscript?
- With so many publishers refusing to consider unsolicited submissions, do I need an agent?
- How can a writer realistically portray the violence of a

harsh world without being overly graphic?
• What are the pros and cons of writing picture books in verse?

This book was written to answer these and many similar questions. It explores the three major types of writing for children—fiction, nonfiction, and picture books—lists the requirements of each field, and describes some of the pitfalls to avoid in your writing. It discusses the basic problems that all writers must solve for themselves: How do you get an idea? Once you have one, how do you develop it into a marketable manuscript? And then, how do you sell the manuscript successfully?

Before getting into that, however, it helps to have a bit of background on the size and scope of the market. Children's book publishing in America is a big business that nets over three billion dollars annually in hardcover sales and  paperback sales. The majority of hardcover sales—perhaps as much as 60%—are made to public and school libraries, but there's an ever-increasing market for juvenile hardcovers as well as paperbacks in mega-book-store chains. Books of all types and for all age groups are in demand, ranging from concept board books covering colors and shapes for one-year-olds to challenging and sometimes controversial novels for teenagers.

To meet this demand, over *six thousand* new juvenile titles are published each year. While the bulk of these are written by established authors, there's room on every children's book publisher's list for newcomers with a fresh and original approach, writers who show promise of developing into the established authors of tomorrow. Perhaps one of these new authors will be you. But first you'll need to decide what you want to say, and to which youthful audience, and then you'll have to learn how to say it in the most effective way possible.

## Finding time; making space

"There's so much I want to write about, but I just can't seem to find the time," is an excuse I often hear from would-be writers. I'm afraid I don't have much patience with it—or them. "You'll never *find* the time to write," I reply. "You'll have to *make* the time, and on a regular basis." No matter how busy you are, there must be a few hours a week that you can devote to your writing.

Those hours will probably involve sacrifices of one kind or another. You may have to decline an appealing invitation to a Sunday brunch with old friends if it cuts into your writing time. Or you may have to miss that fascinating late-night talk show interview if you're going to hold to your self-imposed schedule and get up at five in the morning to work on your children's book.

While it's a good idea to set aside some time to write each day, it often isn't possible, and isn't absolutely necessary. What's more important is to look hard at your weekly schedule and decide on a certain number of hours when—barring vacations or sudden emergencies—you're pretty sure you'll be able to sit at your writing desk. They may add up to two hours on Tuesday, a half hour on Thursday, a full hour on Friday, and another hour on Sunday. It really doesn't matter as long as the schedule is realistic and you hold to it rigorously. Even if you have only three or four hours a week for writing at first, you'll be surprised at how much you can accomplish if you work at it steadily.

Many aspiring writers who hold down full-time jobs claim they don't have enough energy left after their demanding workdays to pursue their writing ambitions seriously. Some make solemn pledges to do so after they've retired. I made similar promises myself while I was working as publisher and editor-in-chief of Clarion Books. But as the years passed, I realized that if I was ever going to be a nonfiction writer I'd better start now.

In the years that followed, I put in an hour or more at my living room desk each morning before leaving for the Clarion office, spent another hour or two doing library research several evenings a week, and looked forward to weekends and vacations when I could devote solid blocks of time to my writing.

The investment paid off. Holding to the above schedule, I managed to produce a nonfiction book every year and had 10 books in print by the time I was ready to take an early retirement from Clarion. This track record gave me the confidence I needed to sustain and expand my writing output after I'd "retired." The proceeds from my writing also helped to cushion the income decline I experienced after leaving my full-time day job.

Besides time to write, authors also need places where they can be alone to concentrate and give unrestricted freedom to their ideas. It doesn't have to be a separate room just for that purpose, and usually isn't. The essential thing is that it be a place where you can be by yourself. And don't be afraid to hang a "Don't Disturb" sign on the door. If you don't take your writing time seriously, no one else in your life will.

## Getting in the mood

After you've settled on a place to write and established a definite writing schedule, how can you best get started? Every author has his own favorite recipe for warming up. Some simply switch on their computer or put a sheet of paper in the typewriter and plunge into notes, an outline, or even Chapter One. Others straighten their desks and sharpen pencils to get into the mood. Still others draw floor plans of the rooms they'll be describing in their novel or sketch the faces and clothes of the main characters.

Whatever works best for you as a trigger, I strongly recommend that you keep a writing notebook and/or a journal. Before I began to write articles for publication, and later juvenile nonfiction books, I used my journal to sharpen my writing skills. I might not pick up the journal for weeks or even months, but when I did I recorded in it the main events in my life, what delighted me and what troubled me. Although I didn't intend for anyone else to read the journal, I tried to organize each entry in the clearest and most effective way, and polished every sentence until its rhythm satisfied me. Keeping such a journal would probably be useful for you, too, if you're not sure how to get started with your writing or are between book projects.

After I began writing books steadily, I maintained my personal journal but also started a series of writing notebooks. Since then they've become a sort of continuing logbook of my writing career. In them I outline books, articles, and lectures, draft complicated letters before typing them, and make lists of my various freelance commitments and when I plan to get to them. You might use a similar workbook or create a computer file to jot down ideas for new novels or picture books as they occur to you, or to write brief character sketches of two teenage girls you overhear on a bus or a little boy you see walking a big dog. You never know when you may be able to weave such an incident into a story.

Although I now write my manuscripts on a computer, I still like to keep notes in longhand in a notebook. However, you may prefer working on a computer and creating individual files for your book, short story, and article ideas, and your personal musings on other writing topics. The important thing is to find a method that you're comfortable with and that enables you to express yourself most freely.

## Studying the competition

Another good use for a notebook or computer file, especially for beginning authors, is for writing brief critiques of children's books you read. I'm always surprised, when I go through a pile of unsolicited submissions in my office or evaluate manuscripts at a writers' conference, by the fact that so many new authors seem almost completely unaware of what's being published in the children's book field today. They may remember a few books they themselves read and loved as children, and some others that they read aloud to their own children 20 years ago. But they obviously haven't taken the trouble to read any *current* children's books before they sat down at their computers. As a consequence, most of their manuscripts are unsuited to today's audience.

Would a doctor perform an operation before learning the newest or latest techniques for that surgery or would a tailor cut out the cloth for a garment without first researching what's in vogue? Obviously, a children's book writer can't expect to be able to dash off a successful story without reading any contemporary children's books. If you'd like expert guidance on what to read, ask your local children's librarian for a list of recommended titles. Or you can go a children's bookstore or browse in the children's department of one of the big chain bookstores. Or see our Suggested Reading List that starts on page 171.

After you've read and thought about a book, you may want to write a brief description of it in your notebook, and analyze where you feel the author succeeded with his plotting and characterization, and where he failed. By doing so, you'll hone your critical skills. You'll also gain some valuable insights into the craft of writing that particular kind of book.

## A case of arrested development?

As you delve into the wide range of contemporary children's literature, from picture books for preschoolers to biographies for middle-grade readers to novels for young teens, begin thinking of where you might fit into the picture as an author. What age group would you feel most comfortable writing for? A juvenile editor I know believes that all children's book authors are cases of arrested development. He's joking, of course, but there may be more than a little truth in his statement. Picture book authors like Kevin Henkes, Charlotte Zolotow, and Marc Brown clearly have a direct link to their memories of what it was like to be five years old, while the agonies of adolescence are as vivid as if they'd happened yesterday to such popular young adult novelists as Walter Dean Myers, Laurie Halse Anderson, Angela Johnson, and Jacqueline Woodson.

Close identification with a particular age group isn't limited to writers of fiction. For example, as an author of nonfiction I often write for the ten-to-twelve-year-old audience, the "intermediate" group, as it's called. I'm convinced that's because those were my happiest years as a child, a time when the world and its history opened up for me and I felt as if I were making an exciting new discovery each day. Now I'm writing out of my memories of that boy and for the thousands of children who, I hope, share his interests and enthusiasms.

In determining which age group is right for you, you might ask yourself some of the following questions: (1) What would I most like to write? A fantasy about a talking pig? An account of the extinction of the dinosaurs? A novel about a girl with a weight problem who's afraid no one will ask her to the prom? (2) Why do I want to work with this material? Does it spring from some of my own experiences, pleasures, fears, or fascinations as a child or adolescent? and (3) What age group do I think would be most interested in my book?

Be honest in your answers. Especially with a first book, don't pretend to be interested in something you're not just because you think it has a better chance of selling. Maybe your friends advised you to write a lengthy fantasy novel in the vein of the Harry Potter books because all the youngsters they know are lapping up such stories. But if you really want to explore the feelings of a lonely little boy in first grade, trust your instincts. A more moving, and saleable, manuscript will probably be the result.

In the course of getting ready to write, many authors wonder if they have the proper equipment. Should they replace their two-year-old computer with an expensive new model, and invest in a better-quality printer? When making your final choices about equipment, just remember one thing: *No pen or typewriter or computer was ever responsible for the success or failure of a manuscript.* A computer may make the process of writing easier, but the strength and appeal of the content depend entirely on you, the writer.

## Getting specific

All right. Let's turn now from general advice to a specific writing situation. Imagine that you're a young man or woman who wants to write for children. It's Tuesday morning at 5:30, and the rest of the family is still asleep. You have an hour-and-a-half before you have to leave for your job in the city or get the children off to school. So you go quietly to the table in the sunroom that you've made into a desk and take out your writing notebook.

In the last few months, you've been reading one children's book after another. After studying them carefully and pondering your own talents and interests, you've decided you'd like to write nonfiction for the upper elementary age group. Now the moment of truth has arrived: You have to settle on an idea to explore. What will it be? As if looking to nature for inspiration, you gaze out the window at the azalea bushes that are about to burst into bloom. Maybe children would be interested in an up-to-date book on gardening.

Where *do* good nonfiction ideas come from, and how can they be shaped into exciting and marketable books? Those are the questions we'll take up and try to answer in the next three chapters.

 Chapter Two

# Nonfiction Goes to the Ball

Youngsters in each new generation have needed to find out the facts about everything for school assignments, or just to satisfy their curiosity. As a result, nonfiction has always been a staple of children's book publishing. And it's interesting to note that the first John Newbery Medal (which recognizes excellence in children's literature) was awarded in 1922 to a work of nonfiction, Hendrik Willem Van Loon's *The Story of Mankind*.

For many years after that, however, nonfiction books tended to be Cinderellas on many publishers' lists. There the books were, sitting quietly in the background with titles like *The Wonders of Light* and *Clara Barton: Civil War Nurse*, while the bulk of the publishers' editorial, design, and promotion efforts were lavished on their fiction and picture book offerings. Juvenile nonfiction also suffered a heavy blow in the 1970s when federal funds for school libraries, probably the largest purchasers of nonfiction books, were sharply reduced. As a consequence, many publishers cut back on the number of new nonfiction titles they issued, and hundreds of solid backlist titles went out of print as sales declined.

This situation reversed itself in the 1980s when Cinderella suddenly found herself invited to a spectacular new nonfiction ball. Schoolchildren still needed informational books, and there were fresh library funds to purchase them in many localities. Expanded children's sections at mega-bookstores provided a new market for juvenile nonfiction, especially for books aimed at preschoolers and early elementary age children.

Perhaps most important, reviewers and librarians began to treat juvenile nonfiction more seriously. *The Boston Globe-Horn Book* children's book awards set up a separate category to recognize the best nonfiction books. The Society of Children's Book Writers and Illustrators initiated a Golden Kite Award for nonfiction and the National Council of Teachers of English established the Orbis Pictus Award to recognize each year's outstanding nonfiction titles. And then, in 1988, the American Library Association awarded the Newbery Medal to Russell Freedman's *Lincoln: A Photobiography*—the first time a nonfiction book had received the coveted Newbery since 1956.

Since 1988 all Newbery Medal winners have been awarded to fiction books. Recognizing that nonfiction deserved more consistent recognition, the A.L.A. in 2001 launched the Robert F. Sibert Informational Book Award, named for the founder of the Bound-to-Stay-Bound pre-bindery that funds the award. The Sibert is presented annually to "the most distinguished American informational book for children published during the preceding year" and offers writers a strong new incentive to produce outstanding nonfiction.

## Series nonfiction: a good place to start

Today, and in the years ahead, all signs point to an even wider range of juvenile nonfiction titles being made available to young readers. Many will appear in series like those published by Enslow Books and Children's Press. These series deal with all sorts of subjects, from the history and geography of each state, to discussions of contemporary social issues such as drugs, to how-to books on various sports, both established and new. If you're interested in doing a book for a series, you should study the publishers' catalogues and publications and then write the editors for information on their plans so that you can see where your idea might fit in.

The series field is an excellent place for a beginning non-fiction writer to get a start. Editors are always on the lookout for new writers who can do in-depth research and turn that research into readable, compelling books. But you'll need to have a flexible attitude if you decide to try your hand at series nonfiction, as the following case history demonstrates.

Some years ago, I worked at a writers' conference with Barbara Kramer, a beginner who had an interesting sample chapter for a book about women lighthouse keepers. At my suggestion, she submitted the chapter to Enslow Books. They weren't interested in the lighthouse project, but liked Kramer's writing style and invited her to submit a sample chapter for a biography of novelist Alice Walker that they wanted to include in one of their series. Demonstrating flexibility, Kramer put aside her book on lighthouse keepers, wrote the sample chapter on Alice Walker, and got a contract to do the book. Since then, Kramer has written 20 more books for Enslow!

Besides series books, many children's publishers offer an equally wide range of individual nonfiction titles for all age groups. There are colorful nonfiction picture books for preschoolers on everything from ants to icebergs; pure science, natural history, holiday, and social history titles for the middle grades; self-help and how-to books for older children and teenagers, popular in both the trade and institutional markets; and biographies for all age groups.

## Close focus, concise text, eye-catching visuals

Whether a nonfiction book is part of a series or an individual title, chances are that it will be conceived and written in a way very different from the one that prevailed even a short while ago. Take, for instance, a book that I edited in the 1970s, *Juvenile Justice* by Willard A. Heaps. This book was typical of many nonfiction titles of its time. Designed for readers of middle school age and up, it presented a broad overview of the entire juvenile justice system from the time a young person commits a crime until his or her case is decided and punishment is determined. The book was 224 pages long; fourteen actual case histories were woven into the text, and it included a list of sources and readings and an index. But it had no illustrations.

*Juvenile Justice* received excellent reviews in the library media, went through four printings, and was counted a solid success. But it's unlikely that a publisher would produce the book in the same style and manner today.

Why not? Because times have changed, and with them the way in which authors and publishers approach juvenile nonfiction topics. If an author were planning a similar book now, he or she would probably team up with a photographer, and they might decide to focus on one day's activities in a typical juvenile court. Or they might follow a single juvenile offender through the whole process, from apprehension, to trial, to disposal of the case.

Whichever course they chose, the basic facts about the juvenile justice system would emerge at appropriate points in the text. But the new manuscript would be tight; instead of over 200 pages, it would probably run to no more than 50 pages. There would be at least one photograph on every double-page spread, and sometimes two or three. And the finished book would be only 64 or 96 pages long.

These hypothetical concepts point up three features that seem to be characteristic of the current approach to juvenile nonfiction, and that authors should keep firmly in mind. They apply to books for all age groups, from preschool picture books to titles aimed at young adults. The three key features are: *1) a close focus on one significant aspect of a topic that will also reveal other aspects; 2) a concise, tightly written text that will catch and hold the interest of young readers; 3) and a built-in emphasis on illustrations, whether they be photographs or drawings, or a combination of the two.* The visual impact of nonfiction is especially important now, when books have to compete with so many other media for a young person's attention.

## Getting the idea

Despite the new emphasis on the visual in all types of juvenile nonfiction, the text—however brief—is still the key factor that determines the form of any book. And every good text begins with a good idea. Such ideas come from many different sources, depending on the author's personal background, interests, and areas of expertise.

For example, when Russell Freedman attended an exhibit of photographs of turn-of-the-century immigrant children at the New-York Historical Society, he was moved by their lively, animated expressions despite the harsh conditions in which many of them lived and worked. The pictures made him think of his grandparents and other relatives who had emigrated to the United States from Eastern Europe at about the same time. From this museum visit came the idea for Freedman's striking nonfiction book, *Immigrant Kids.*

Caroline Arnold got the idea for her book, *Pets Without Homes,* when she read an article in a Los Angeles newspaper about a young veterinarian who visited area schools, telling youngsters about her work in an animal shelter and bringing along some of the shelter's furry residents for the children to see and play with. Arnold, who had a science background and had written a number of books on scientific subjects, thought children would be interested in reading about what goes on in a typical animal shelter. She contacted the veterinarian and a new book was under way.

The author took the idea a step further, however, before she began the actual writing. Aware of the illustration possibilities in the material, she decided the book would make a good photo essay. The term *photo essay* came into use in the 1970s to describe a type of nonfiction book for middle-grade children and older readers in which the illustrations, usually photographs, play as important a role as the text, and must be of equally high quality. Once Arnold had settled on a photo-essay approach, she got in touch with Richard Hewett, the professional photographer she had worked with on other books, to see if he would be interested in collaborating with her on the project. He was enthusiastic about the idea, and together they developed *Pets Without Homes* from that point on.

Sometimes the idea for a nonfiction book comes along when an author least expects it. That's what happened to me in the case of my book, *Chimney Sweeps*. I was flying to Oklahoma City on business when the plane stopped in Chicago and a tall, rangy young man carrying what I thought was a musical instrument case took the seat next to me. We started to talk, and I discovered that the man—whose name was Christopher Curtis—was a chimney sweep, and his case contained samples of the special brushes for cleaning chimneys that he manufactured at his own small factory in Vermont. He was on his way to Oklahoma City to conduct a seminar for local sweeps on how to clean chimneys more efficiently.

Curtis went on to tell me a little about the history of chimney sweeping and its revival as a profession in recent years. In turn, I told him I was a writer of children's books, and that he'd fired my interest in chimney sweeps as a possible subject. We exchanged business cards, and a month or so later I wrote to tell him that I'd followed up on the idea and had started researching the book on chimney sweeps. I asked him if he'd be willing to read the manuscript for accuracy. He agreed to do so and volunteered to supply photographs of present day sweeps that could be used (and were) as illustrations in the book.

According to an old English superstition, it's lucky to meet a chimney sweep. Well, meeting Christopher Curtis was certainly lucky for me!

## The "levels" test

After you have an idea for a book, the next thing to do is test it to see if it's worth pursuing. But first you should ask yourself a blunt question: Is this an idea to which I want to devote a year or more of my life? For it takes most authors at least six months to research a nonfiction book and another six months to write and rewrite it. That's a major commitment of time and energy, and not one to be made lightly.

If your answer is "yes," you should go on to examine the idea carefully and see if it has enough *levels* to make a good book. What do I mean by levels? Look at the idea for *Immigrant Kids*. Not only did it offer Russell Freedman the opportunity to explore the life of children in another time, but it also gave him a chance to investigate the dramatic story of American immigration, a subject every child studies in school at one time or another.

Or take *Chimney Sweeps*. When I got into preliminary research for that book, I discovered that besides the obvious human interest centering on the plight of child sweeps in nineteenth-century England, the subject touched on architectural and economic history, and it had played an important role in the passage of the first laws against child labor. Weaving these different levels together made *Chimney Sweeps* more interesting to write—and I believe it made it more interesting for readers also.

Once your idea has passed the "levels" test, the next step is to check R. R. Bowker's annual *Subject Guide to Children's*

*Books in Print*, available in the reference department of most libraries, to see what else is available on the subject. Or you can go on the Internet and investigate what competing titles are listed there. When I looked up "chimney sweeps," I was pleased to find that no other nonfiction treatments were in print. But when I looked up "skyscrapers" in preparation for *The Skyscraper Book*, I was dismayed to see six other books listed. Upon examining the books, though, I realized that several of them were written for the picture book audience, whereas I intended mine for the 8 to 12 age group, and all of the books focused on how skyscrapers were constructed, while I planned to emphasize why and by whom they were built.

## Choosing age & slant

This brings up the importance of deciding on the right age group and slant for your nonfiction idea. Often a subject such as skyscrapers can be treated for either preschoolers or upper elementary and middle school readers; which you choose to write for may depend on what else is available, or your inclinations as a writer, or both.

By the same token, a subject like skyscrapers can be approached from many different angles. The trick is to find one compatible with your interests and skills that doesn't merely duplicate existing material. If you succeed in coming up with that combination, public and school librarians will probably find room in their budgets for your book, even if they already have several other books on the same subject.

After weighing your idea carefully and examining the competition, the time will come when you'll have to decide whether or not to proceed. Try to be as honest as possible with yourself at this point; it'll save you a lot of trouble and disappointment later. If you feel the idea just isn't large enough for a book, don't despair. It may provide the basis for an excellent children's magazine article. If, on the other hand, you're more convinced than ever that it has the makings of a book, new questions arise. Should you research and write the entire manuscript before approaching a publisher, or should you query first to find out if an editor is interested in your idea?

If you're a beginner, a combination of the two would probably be the best course to take. You should do enough research to make sure there's sufficient material for a book. Then you'll need to write a full outline and draft one or two sample chapters to show how you intend to treat the subject. After that, you can send query letters to publishers and ask if they'd like to see your outline and chapters.

## Writing a nonfiction query letter or proposal

Some query letters for nonfiction books strain for a dramatic beginning: "Can you imagine the devastation that would result if a major new earthquake struck southern California?" Others go on for four or five single-spaced typewritten pages in which every section of every chapter is described in minute detail.

As an editor, I tend to tune out on such letters, for I like a query letter to be factual, to the point, and no more than a page long. Teaser openings don't work with me; I prefer a straightforward approach like that in the following example:

> Dear Mr. Giblin:
>
> I have spent the last year researching the life of Mary Todd Lincoln and have just completed the outline and three sample chapters of a proposed biography of her for ages 10 to 14. Much has been written for this age group about Abraham Lincoln, of course, including Russell Freedman's excellent biography. But after going on the Internet and checking the latest edition of the *Subject Guide to Children's Books in Print*—and talking with our

local school and public librarians—I could find only two other books about Mrs. Lincoln, and both came out quite some time ago. In my sample chapters, I have tried to deal honestly with the complexities of Mary Lincoln's character, and have not concealed or whitewashed the neurotic side of her personality. However, in many other respects I consider her to be a heroine who played an important role during one of the most difficult periods in our history. Certainly she is a woman young readers should know about.

I have previously published biographical articles for children in *Cricket* and *Highlights*, but this is my first attempt at a book. Would you like to see my sample material? I enclose a stamped, self-addressed envelope for your convenience in replying.

That sort of query letter would get a favorable response from me—and I imagine from most editors—because the author obviously has a thoughtful, professional attitude. And, after reading the outline and sample chapters, we might feel confident enough about the project to offer him or her a contract. At that point, buoyed by our commitment, the author would be ready to proceed with in-depth research.

Once an author has become established as a nonfiction writer, the submission procedure is different. Then, instead of doing an outline and sample chapters and querying editors, the author writes a *proposal* for a book and sends it to an editor. What exactly is a proposal? Basically a two- or three-page description of the future book, indicating what the subject will be and how the author intends to treat it. Perhaps a sample of text, or a brief outline, or both will be included. If illustrations are to be an important element, that should be mentioned in the proposal, along with the author's ideas for them—photographs, drawings, etc.

Since the editor usually knows the author's work and reputation, the proposal will be enough for him to decide whether or not the project seems right for his list. If his decision is "yes," the established author—like the beginner—will then move on to the research stage.

 Chapter Three

# Researching, Outlining, and Writing a Juvenile Nonfiction Book

**E**ach book demands its own research approach, and you have to discover it as you go along. With most subjects, the Internet and a good library will be your first stops. As preparation, you should have in hand a list of topics that relate to your main subject. Investigating these will help you to discover the various levels in the material that were discussed in the preceding chapter.

When I was researching *Chimney Sweeps* at the New York Public Library, for example, I naturally turned first to "Chimney Sweeps and Sweeping" and jotted down all the relevant titles and their call numbers. But I didn't stop there. Realizing that I would need to know the history of chimneys and their development, I looked up "Chimneys" next. And since chimney sweeping was an early and glaring example of child labor, I turned to that subject heading also. By the time I was finished, I had begun to build a sizable bibliography.

I wrote *Chimney Sweeps* before I began to work on a computer. If I were researching the book today, I'd start by going on the Internet to see what I could find concerning the topics mentioned above. Then I'd print out the information I discovered and, if relevant books were cited, make a list of the titles to seek out in a library or bookstore. While the Internet is crammed with valuable material, I've found much of what's on it is superficial and sometimes unreliable. When it comes to accurate, in-depth information, I still prefer delving into books.

Once I've had a chance to examine the books, I set out to buy the ones that seem to contain the most relevant and useful information for my purposes. I like the freedom that comes from having my own copies to write in, highlight, and sometimes question. If the books are out-of-print, I use a search engine to locate copies at online bookstores.

## "I was there" resources

As you pursue your research, it's a good idea to emphasize primary sources—first-person accounts by people who were present at a particular event: letters, diaries, or historical documents like the Parliamentary investigations into the living and working conditions of British climbing boys that I found for *Chimney Sweeps*.

A particularly good example of the use of primary source material is Jim Murphy's prize-winning book *The Boys' War*. It draws on letters and diaries written by young Union and Confederate soldiers to give readers a vivid, firsthand picture of what it was like to fight in the Civil War.

But sometimes no "I was there" material is available, and you'll have to rely on secondary sources: articles and books written long after the fact. Then you'll need to keep your antennae up in order to catch those windy generalities that so often mask a lack of knowledge, or the inclusion of statistics and other historical data that, for one reason or another, arouse your suspicions.

In doing research I—along with most juvenile nonfiction authors—feel a special responsibility to my young readers, for I know that my book may be the first they will have read on the subject. Consequently, I try to check each fact against *at least two other sources* before including it in the text. Such double—and triple-checking can turn up myths that have long passed as truths. For instance, while researching *Fireworks, Picnics, and Flags*, I read two books that said an old bell-ringer sat in the tower of Independence Hall almost all day on July 4, 1776. He was waiting for word that independence had been declared so that he could ring the Liberty Bell.

At last, in late afternoon, a small boy ran up the steps of the tower and shouted, "Ring, Grandfather! Ring for Liberty!" The old man did so at once, letting all of Philadelphia know that America was no longer a British colony. It makes a fine story; however, according to the third source I checked, it's apocryphal and appeared for the first time in a mid-nineteenth century textbook titled *Myths and Legends of the Revolution*. Knowing that, I still included it in my book—but I presented it as a good yarn, not a true story.

## Up close and personal

One of the best ways to immerse yourself in the background of your subject, whether it be historical or contemporary, is to visit the sites where the events took place. For *Fireworks, Picnics, and Flags*, I spent two days at Independence National Historical Park in Philadelphia, toured Independence Hall, visited the rented rooms nearby where Thomas Jefferson drafted the Declaration of Independence, and watched a group of awed third-graders touch the Liberty Bell in its pavilion. All of these experiences enabled me to infuse the text with lively, firsthand details that I couldn't have obtained from any book or article.

Russell Freedman is a great believer in on-site research. In his Newbery acceptance speech for *Lincoln*, he said:

> "There's something magic about being able to lay your eyes on the real thing—something you can't get from your reading alone. As I sat at my desk in New York City and described Lincoln's arrival in New Salem, Illinois, at the age of 22, I could picture the scene in my mind's eye because I

had walked down those same dusty lanes, where
cattle still graze behind split-rail fences and geese
flap about underfoot."

Personal interviews are another way of enlivening your
nonfiction book with unique, firsthand material. They can
help make a complex scientific subject clear and exciting for
your readers, as did Caroline Arnold's interviews with pale-
ontologists at the Los Angeles Page Museum in preparation
for her photo essay, *Trapped in Tar: Fossils from the Ice Age.*
Or they can give you a better perspective on recent developments in a particular field, which was the upshot of my interview with the head of the Milk Safety Branch of the
Department of Agriculture when I was researching *Milk: The
Fight for Purity.*

Today it is increasingly acceptable to set up interviews
by email and to submit questions and areas for discussion in
advance. It is also increasingly acceptable to conduct telephone interviews, especially if your respondent is hundreds
or thousands of miles away. When conducting telephone
interviews, never use a speaker-phone. A better alternative
is to record the conversation with a suction-cup microphone
available from any electronics store, after—of course—asking
your subject for permission to record the session.

For in-person interviews, most authors today use small,
unobtrusive tape recorders. But I, like some other writers,
still prefer to take notes by hand in a pocket notebook. I find
this method gives me a better chance to clarify points as the
interview progresses, and to jot down only what seems significant, whereas, in editing transcribed tapes, I've often felt
as if I were plowing through a mound of useless material
before I came to any gems. Other writers do both, taping the
interview for future reference while jotting down significant
points for followup as they proceed.

Whenever I go out on a research expedition, whether it's

to a library or an actual site, I always take along a supply of ruled 4" x 6" cards. At the top I write the subject for handy reference later when I file the cards alphabetically in a metal box. I also write the title, author, publisher, and date of the book I'm reading so that I'll have all that information on hand when I compile the bibliography and source notes for the book.

By no means will all of the facts I take down appear in the finished book. Only a small part of any author's research shows up in the final manuscript. But I think a reader can feel the presence of the rest beneath the surface, lending substance and authority to the writing.

## Back matter, the index, and "extras"

Many juvenile nonfiction books contain special sections at the back, known as the "back matter." It's good to decide what you want to include in the back matter at the research stage and begin assembling the necessary information. For example, in *Walls: Defenses Throughout History*, I decided early on that a glossary of unfamiliar terms would be helpful, so whenever I came across a new term or word, I jotted down the definition. When the manuscript of the book was finished, I put all the definitions together in alphabetical order for the glossary.

Teachers and others working with children appreciate such extensions of a book's basic text. Including William Blake's poem, "The Chimney Sweeper," at the end of *Chimney Sweeps* drew praise, and a librarian told me that a favorite feature in *The Skyscraper Book* was the section at the back entitled, "Fabulous Facts about Famous Skyscrapers," which was a listing of hard-to-believe statistics about the Empire State Building, the Sears Tower, and other lofty structures. So keep the possibility of "extras" such as these in mind as you proceed with the research for your book. Well-chosen back matter can give the book added depth and help it to stand out above the competition.

Another feature that almost all juvenile nonfiction books should include is an index, but it can be compiled only after the book has been typeset and put into pages. And, since indexing requires special skills, in the past it has been done by a professional indexer rather than the author. However, the recent availability of indexing software programs has made it easier for authors to be part of the process. In any case, it's not something you'll have to be concerned about until you complete your manuscript.

## Biographies: full-scale portraits

There was a time not so long ago when it was hard to tell what was true and what was false in many juvenile biographies. The books were filled with unsubstantiated passages of dialogue, emphasized the subjects' youthful years, and ignored the more painful aspects of their lives. For example, the highly regarded picture book biography of George Washington by Ingri and Parin D'Aulaire glossed over the fact that Washington was a slaveowner, and their biography of Abraham Lincoln ended before his assassination.

The texts of biographies for older children tended to be wordy, and only a few pages were devoted to illustrations. These were generally undistinguished line drawings or poorly reproduced photographs. Some older level biographies contained indexes, but almost none included extensive bibliographies or source notes. The reader had to go on faith alone when it came to judging the author's reliability.

Today all this has changed. School and public librarians—the most important customers for hardcover children's biographies—will no longer tolerate fictionalized dialogue in the books, and they prefer to have all quotations documented, either in footnotes or in a list of sources at the back. They fault biographies, even picture book treatments for young children, that don't offer full-scale portraits of their subjects. And they expect biographies for all age groups to be well-designed and illustrated.

## Accentuate the positive

What methods can authors of juvenile biographies employ in order to deal with these requirements? Here are a few suggestions:

1. Include incidents from the subject's childhood and youth with which young readers can identify, but concentrate on the adult accomplishments that make the person worthy of anyone's attention.

2. Avoid the temptation to invent dialogue and use instead extracts from letters, speeches, recollections, and other documents to bring the subject to life. Remember to make a note of where you found each quotation so that you can put this information in your source notes.

3. Don't be afraid to discuss the blemishes on the subject's personality and character. They'll make his or her virtues stand out more sharply by contrast, and result in a convincing, three-dimensional portrait. For example, in his biography *Franklin Delano Roosevelt*, Russell Freedman acknowledges the existence of Lucy Mercer, Roosevelt's longtime mistress, without dwelling on that side of the President's life. The latter points up one of the main differences between juvenile and adult biographies. Instead of emphasizing the subject's failings, as do many adult biographers, the children's biographer admits the person's faults but accentuates his or her positive qualities.

There's an exception to this rule. If you're writing about an out-and-out villain, as I did in the Sibert Award winner, *The Life and Death of Adolf Hitler*, you'll need to find at least a few human traits in the subject to help set off his or her monstrous acts. If you don't, the portrayal runs the risk of seeming superficial if not downright unbelievable.

You walk a tricky line, though, in trying to make someone like Adolf Hitler understandable without evoking sympathy for him. In Hitler's case, I felt his rejection three times by a prestigious Viennese art school, and his subsequent bitterness, helped explain why he was attracted to a destructive organization like the National Socialist (Nazi) Party. But at the same time I was careful to show that his youthful resentments in no way excused his later heinous atrocities.

4. Write the text fully and with a sense of the dramatic, but keep it as succinct as possible so that there'll be room for plenty of illustrations. The latter is especially important if you're planning to write a picture book biography.

## Picture book biographies

A few picture book biographies, like those written and illustrated by the D'Aulaires, have long been available. But only in the last several decades has the genre come into its own, pioneered by such authors and author-illustrators as Diane Stanley, David Adler, Kathleen Krull, and Don Brown. They and their perceptive editors recognized that young readers no longer reject as "babyish" nonfiction books published in a picture book format. Accustomed to getting much of their information from visual sources like television and the Internet, beginning readers welcome biographies that allot as much or more space to the illustrations as they do to the text. As a result, picture book biographies are now read and enjoyed by children as young as seven and as old as fourteen.

I was eager to try my hand at this type of book, and entered the field with brief biographies of several of the Founding Fathers—George Washington, Thomas Jefferson, and Benjamin Franklin. It wasn't long before I discovered how hard it was to create a portrait of meaning and substance within the physical limitations of the picture book format.

Here, drawn from my experience, are some suggestions of ways to meet the challenges if you decide to try your own hand at a picture book biography.

1. First, you should choose a subject that will appeal—and be understandable—to both elementary and middle school readers. Benjamin Franklin was a good candidate for such treatment, but Adolf Hitler probably wouldn't be.

2. Be braced for the fact that you'll need to do as much research as you would for a longer biography. I spent over a year on the research for the Franklin biography, although the eight-page first draft took just 10 days to write.

3. While doing the research, keep an eye out for a strong narrative line that will tie the text together. In my biography of Franklin, this line turned out to be Ben's on-and-off relationship with his only living son, William, who remained loyal to Great Britain even as his father was helping to draft the Declaration of Independence.

4. Search, too, for anecdotes that bring the subject to life in ways that can be appreciated by younger as well as older readers. In the Franklin book, for example, I wanted to convey his love of life—and of wine and women—to a wide range of young readers. At the same time, I wanted the book to be acceptable to the adults who would be buying it for their libraries and schools, or for their own children.

In pursuit of these goals, here's how I described Ben's first trip to England as a youth of eighteen. "He found work with a London printer and spent his free time exploring the great city and reading all the latest books. He had his share of fun, too, going to pubs with his friends and flirting with the pretty girls he met."

5. Once the research is done, you'll face another problem: how to compress the mass of material you've gathered into a text of no more than 10 or so manuscript pages. My only advice in this regard is to always keep in mind the key incidents that are needed to tell your subject's story. And be prepared to jettison those that aren't absolutely essential, no matter how much you may like them.

6. As you write, you should remember that the artist will need a variety of scenes to illustrate. For example, you wouldn't want to have a stretch of text in which the subject does nothing but make speeches. In *Franklin*, I deliberately broke up a description of Ben's work as ambassador to the French court with an account of a hot-air balloon ascent that he attended in Paris.

7. Finally, you should make good use of the back matter pages at the end of the book for items that there isn't room for in the main text. In *Franklin*, my editor and I found room at the back for a timeline of the main events in Franklin's long and productive life, brief descriptions of his most important inventions, a sampling of his familiar—and some of his less familiar—sayings, and a full index.

## Next step: the visuals

When the text of a picture book biography has been written and revised to everyone's satisfaction, the writer's work is essentially done and the manuscript moves on to the illustrator that the editor has selected. That's not true of nonfiction books for older readers. Unless you're working with a photographer on a photo essay, you'll probably be expected to research and assemble any photographic illustrations that are needed for an older level nonfiction book. Along with photographs, such illustrations may include reproductions of historic cartoons, posters, and drawings and paintings from museums, but not original drawings or maps; the latter are usually the publisher's responsibility.

You may be able to negotiate an arrangement whereby the publisher agrees to assume the print and permission costs for the illustrations up to a limit of, say, $2,000 or $3,000, but you'll be responsible for the balance. That doesn't mean you should try to cut corners. In my experience, the better the illustrations in a book, the more successful it is in the marketplace.

# Picture research: playing detective

Doing picture research is a little like playing detective. Both involve a combination of intuition and logic, with a bit of luck thrown in for good measure. I begin by making up a wish list of the illustrations I'd ideally like to have for each chapter in the book and then making a matching list of likely sources. After that the search begins.

Following this procedure with *Charles A. Lindbergh: A Human Hero*, I began with two research trips, one to St. Paul, Minnesota, the other to Washington, D.C. I'd read that Lindbergh, a native of Minnesota, had left the photo albums from his childhood and youth to the Minnesota Historical Society in St. Paul, and I wanted to go through them. In Washington, I was confident the photo collections of the Air and Space Museum, the Library of Congress, and the National Archives would be full of vivid pictures of Lindbergh's nonstop flight to Paris in 1927 and his later career.

Today, before planning the trips, I'd do preliminary research on the Internet to see what was available in the various collections. Perhaps I'd even be able to order prints of the pictures I wanted online, thus avoiding the travel expenses the trips would entail. But I'm a great believer in serendipity, and the unexpected discoveries one often makes on the spot, so I'd probably still take the trips. But I might not have to stay as long because of the earlier research I'd done on the Internet.

Although I gathered a lot of remarkable pictures for the Lindbergh biography in St. Paul and Washington, there were still sections in the manuscript that lacked illustrations. To fill the gaps, most of which concerned the kidnapping of the Lindbergh baby, the trial of the kidnapper, and Lindbergh's later involvement with the Isolationist organization "America First," I turned to commercial photo agencies in New York. When I was finally finished, I found I had more pictures than could be used in the book. But that was all right; as with the text research, it's always better to have too much material to work with than too little.

Assembling the illustrations for *Charles Lindbergh* and my other books has taught me several important things about doing picture research. The first is: Never start with the well-known commercial agencies. They charge high reproduction fees which are likely to break your illustration budget. Instead, try to think of other possible sources, such as federal or state agencies like the National Archives and the Minnesota Historical Society that supply photographs for the cost of the prints. Or you might turn to art and natural history museums, which charge modest fees; or to national tourist offices, which are usually glad to give you photographs free of charge, asking only that you credit them in the book's acknowledgments.

Manufacturers of various products are another good source of free photos. Their public relations departments will be happy to send you photographs of everything from tractors to inflatable vinyl scarecrows in return for an acknowledgment in your book.

Wherever you obtain the photos, though, be sure they're of the highest possible quality. There's no point in submitting pictures to your publisher that are scratched, faded, or poorly composed, because they simply won't be usable. The only exception to this rule would be rare or historical photographs, as was the case with some of the family snapshots that appeared in *Charles Lindbergh*.

## Outlining, writing, and re-writing

Once the bulk of the text research is complete and while you're still working on the picture research, you can begin the actual writing of the book. When I reach this stage, I generally draft a rough outline of the entire book, divided into chapters. I do this entirely from memory, without looking at any of the marked-up books or the research cards in the file box. In this way, I can sum up what all the notes, assembled during a year or more of research, have meant to me, and start to give the material my own shape and direction.

Next, I carefully reread the research material for the beginning of the book and make a detailed outline for Chapter One in my writing notebook. After that's done I'm ready to turn on the computer. But first I spread out on the worktable around it all of the books and notes I'll need to refer to as I'm writing. Once I start, I try to keep a momentum going, but often I have to stop to check a date or some other fact. If I have all my reference sources handy, it's easier to get the flow going again after I've solved the problem.

Achieving a consistent personal voice in a nonfiction book requires considerable effort. Often I rewrite a sentence or paragraph three or four times before I'm satisfied enough to move on. In the revisions, I try to make certain the organization is logical and interesting, and smooth out any spots where the style of the original research source is too much in evidence. If you're not careful, there's a danger you'll inadvertently use another writer's wording and then you may be charged with plagiarism if you're careless in not properly marking quotations in hand-written notes.

I'm often asked if I think of the child reader while I'm writing, and my answer is both "yes" and "no." Whenever I come to a new topic in the text, or the mention of a historical event such as the French Revolution or the fall of the Roman Empire, I stop and ask myself, "Will readers have enough prior knowledge of this subject?" If I think they won't, I gear my writing accordingly in an attempt to provide them with the information they will need to understand what I'm saying.

At the same time, I'm careful not to talk down to readers by using oversimple language that may insult their intelligence. For I firmly believe that in nonfiction, as in other types of writing for children, it never hurts to use an occasional "hard" word as long as it's appropriate. That's one of the best ways, after all, to stretch a child's—or anyone's—vocabulary.

As I'm writing, I always try to make the most of the dramatic possibilities in the material. And I deliberately employ fiction techniques of scene-setting and atmosphere-building whenever they seem valid. We'll take a look at some of these techniques in the next chapter.

 Chapter Four

# A Nonfiction Writer
# Is a Storyteller

People are sometimes startled when I say that a nonfiction writer is a storyteller. Aren't nonfiction books and articles made up entirely of facts? Yes, of course. But the organizing and shaping of those facts into readable, interesting prose requires all the skills of a storyteller.

It begins with the idea. Unless the idea has an element of story, of mystery in it, the writer may not be compelled to invest the time and energy needed to develop it.

One Christmas season I happened to see a picture of our plump, jolly Santa Claus in juxtaposition with his tall, thin ancestor, St. Nicholas. My curiosity was aroused: How did two such dissimilar figures become joined? The result was my book, *The Truth About Santa Claus*. Several years later, as I was eating dinner in a restaurant, I found myself wondering when people first began to use spoons, knives, and forks. That, in turn, led me to write *From Hand to Mouth*, which traces the story of our common eating utensils.

There's that word again: story. With each of these book ideas, I was moved to explore the story behind something, whether it was our favorite gift-bringer, or the common, everyday table fork. And it was the lure of the story, and the promise of discovering the key to it, that sustained my interest through the long hours of research.

As I do research, I'm always on the lookout for dramatic or amusing anecdotes that will help to bring the subject to life for young readers. For example, when I was researching *From Hand to Mouth* I was delighted to find the following anecdote, which tells how table knives came to be rounded.

> The design of table knives changed even more noticeably in the seventeenth century. Now that people throughout Europe were eating with forks, they no longer needed knives with sharp points to spear their food. Consequently, by the end of the century most European table knives were made with rounded ends.
>
> Some say Cardinal Richelieu, a French religious and political leader, was responsible for this change in knife design. The Cardinal frequently entertained a nobleman who was in the habit of picking his teeth with the point of his knife. Disgusted with the man's behavior, the Cardinal had the points of all his table knives ground down, and others in the French court followed the Cardinal's lead.

## Discovering the narrative line

As the research begins to take shape, I frequently discover an overall narrative line in the material and build the structure of the book around it. The book *Walls: Defenses Throughout History* began as simply an account of fascinating walls I'd seen, among them Hadrian's Wall and the Great Wall of China. But it grew first into a history of fortifications and then into a demonstration that no defensive wall, from the Great Wall to the Maginot Line, has ever really worked.

*From Hand to Mouth* assumed a circular pattern. It opens on a scene of ancient people eating with their fingers and ends with people once again relying on their fingers in today's fast-food establishments. In between we get glimpses of all the elaborate table manners that came into being with the use of knives, spoons, forks, and chopsticks.

Neither of these patterns—these narrative lines—was imposed on the books in question. They emerged naturally the deeper I got into the research and the more connections I saw between the various aspects of the topic and the way they had changed over time. When critics talk of an informational book being well-organized, I think what they're really referring to is a sense of inner-connectedness and thematic progression. It's as crucial to the success of a nonfiction book, I feel, as a strong plot is to a novel.

Once the overall direction has been determined, and a preliminary outline drafted, the book can be divided into chapters. Here pace is paramount. Often what I originally thought would be one chapter contains too much information and works better if it is divided into two. Ideally, I aim for no more than 10 typewritten pages per chapter, and preferably seven or eight, in order to keep the narrative moving right along. Most of my books for eight-to-eleven-year-olds have run to eight or ten chapters, resulting in final manuscripts of 50 to 90 pages. That length allows room for illustrations and doesn't seem too formidable to today's young readers, who are confronted with so many different media claims on their attention.

My books for older readers of 11 and up, such as the biographies of Charles Lindbergh and Adolf Hitler, are considerably longer. Like my books for younger readers, their chapters are usually no more than 10 manuscript pages in length. But more chapters are required to give a full account of the subjects' lives—23 in the Lindbergh book, 25 in the study of Hitler. The older level books are as heavily illustrated as the younger ones, though, with a photo, map, poster, or political cartoon on almost every other page.

## Chapter titles and openings

Whether they appear in a younger or older level book,

intriguing chapter titles provide another way to encourage a youngster to keep on reading. Sometimes a straightforward, factual title, such as "Walls of World War II" (used in my book *Walls*) works best. Never miss a chance for humor, either, if it's appropriate to the subject, as in the chapter about European table manners before the introduction of forks in *From Hand to Mouth*. I called it "Don't Put Your Whole Hand in the Pot!" In other cases, a more dramatic approach seems called for, like "Hitler Lives," the title of the concluding chapter in the Hitler biography that deals with the alarming rise of neo-Nazism.

The opening paragraphs of each chapter—and especially the first chapter—should be as intriguing as you can make them, for they may well determine whether the reader will go any farther in the book. Try not to begin a chapter with a flat, factual statement, but start instead with an anecdote or scene that will help establish the mood and draw the reader in.

For example, the opening of *The Riddle of the Rosetta Stone* might have begun with a simple statement of fact:

> The Rosetta Stone played a vital role in help-
> ing us understand the literature, politics, and
> social organization of ancient Egypt.

Instead I decided to try to interest youngsters by leading them up to the Stone in its museum setting today. Here is how Chapter One begins:

> The place: The Egyptian Sculpture Gallery of the
> British Museum in London. The time: now. Near the
> entrance to the long, high-ceilinged room stand two
> magnificent granite statues of Pharaoh Amenophis
> III, who ruled Egypt about 1400 B.C. Farther on is a
> colossal head of Pharaoh Ramesses II dating back
> to 1250 B.C. And beyond it, resting on a simple

base, is a slab of black basalt, a volcanic rock.

Next to the statues and the head, the slab seems unimpressive at first glance. It is roughly the size of a tabletop—three feet nine inches long, two feet four and a half inches wide, and eleven inches thick. But many experts would say that this rather small piece of rock was more valuable than any of the larger objects in the room. For it is the famed Rosetta Stone, which gave nineteenth-century scholars their first key to the secrets of ancient Egypt.

I try to achieve a similar dramatic effect with all of my chapter openings but I don't always succeed. If, as is sometimes the case, the material resists dramatization, it's better not to force the issue, but to settle for a more direct, straightforward opening. Opportunities for drama are bound to come up later in the chapter.

## Multicultural dimensions: a richer reading experience

Whenever possible, I like to include information about the contributions of non-Western peoples to the subject under discussion. This adds a multicultural dimension to the book—something all teachers and children's librarians are actively seeking today. *From Hand to Mouth*, for example, features a chapter on chopsticks and how to use them, and I've heard that this chapter has led to classroom exercises in schools from California to New Jersey.

Several other books of mine contain multicultural material. *Let There Be Light: A Book About Windows* describes the unusual ways people have found to bring light and air into their dwellings in Africa, the Middle East, and Asia, as well as in Europe and America. *Be Seated: A Book About*

*Chairs* has a chapter on the elaborately carved ceremonial stools and chairs found in many West African nations. And in *The Truth About Unicorns*, along with an account of the traditional European unicorn, there is a description of the very different Chinese unicorn—the gentle *ki-lin* which embodies Buddhist ideals.

If you can extend your nonfiction books in similar multicultural directions, you'll provide youngsters with a richer reading experience. You'll also enhance the books' chances of being used in the classroom and in multicultural library programs.

## Quotations to enliven text

While most reviewers and librarians are opposed to the use of invented dialogue in juvenile nonfiction, a writer of informational books can almost always enliven the text with well-chosen quotations and extracts from actual conversations. These can be humorous, like the precepts from Erasmus's sixteenth-century book on manners, titled *On Civility in Children*, that I quoted in *From Hand to Mouth*. Here are a few examples: "Take the first piece of meat or fish that you touch, and don't poke around in the pot for a bigger one." "Don't pick your nose when eating and then reach for more food." "Don't throw bones you have chewed back in the pot. Put them on the table or toss them on the floor."

Or the quotations can be impassioned, like the words of Adolf Hitler as the Allied armies closed in on Germany in January, 1945. "I know the war is lost," Hitler confided to a henchman one night during an air raid. Sinking into depression, he muttered, "I'd like most of all to put a bullet through my head." But then he regained his determination. "We'll not capitulate. Never!" he said. "We may go down, but we'll take a world with us.

Often a quotation will contain several relevant sentences but be too long and complicated to hold the interest of young readers. In such cases, it is perfectly permissible to shorten the quotes, as long as all omitted words are shown by ellipses (. . .).

Are permissions required for the use of such quotations? Not if the speaker quoted lived long ago, like Erasmus. Permission is usually not required for the use of quotations by more contemporary figures, either, especially if they're a matter of public record in a newspaper or magazine, and are less than 150 words. As for quotations that come from personal interviews, it's simple courtesy to offer to show the person how you've worked his or her material into your text. This will also serve to forestall any later claims that the person was misquoted.

## Planting a hook

Crucial as the chapter opening is in getting a reader into the chapter, the ending is equally so in summing up its content and pointing the way toward the next chapter. A novelist often plants a dramatic hook or question in the last paragraph of a chapter, and so do many nonfiction writers.

The hook can be designed to pique the reader's curiosity, like this chapter ending in *From Hand to Mouth*:

> The Industrial Revolution, which started in England in the late 1700s, would spur the growth of mass production, including the manufacture of table utensils. And the people of a new nation, the United States of America, would develop their own unique way of using those utensils.

Or the hook can generate suspense, like the following chapter ending from *Charles A. Lindbergh*. Charles and his wife Anne are near the end of a three-month flight to Alaska and the Far East when word comes that Anne's father, Dwight Morrow, has died back home in the United States.

Here is how the chapter ends:

> The Lindberghs booked immediate passage on an ocean liner bound from Shanghai to Seattle. It would be two years before they made another long flight in the repaired Sirius [the Lindberghs' plane]. Two years during which they would face a more challenging test than anything that had happened on their Pacific trip.

There's only one thing no climactic chapter hook should ever do: promise something the following chapter doesn't deliver. That isn't playing fair with the reader.

## The final chapter

The narrative techniques I've described so far—the overall direction of the book, careful pacing, lively quotations and anecdotes, effective chapter openings and closings—all build, of course, toward the last chapter.

In fiction, this chapter contains the climax of the story and the resolution of its major conflicts. So does the concluding chapter of a nonfiction book, but instead of tying up the plot it usually features a summary of the book's content and a final statement of its theme.

This statement can have a thoughtful tone, like the final paragraph in *George Washington*:

> George Washington left behind no children of his own. Instead he left a nation. A nation that he had served as its first Commander-in-Chief, and then as its first President. That is why he is known as the "Father of His Country."

Or the tone can be lighter, like the final sentences in *From Hand to Mouth*. (They follow a discussion of the fact that more and more Japanese today are using knives, forks, and spoons, while many Americans are trying to eat with chopsticks.)

> What's likely is that people in both East and West will continue to experiment with one another's table utensils. And who knows? Perhaps in time they will find a common solution to that age-old problem: how to get food as swiftly, gracefully, and neatly as possible from plate to mouth.

Or the ending can be solemn, like the concluding paragraphs in *When Plague Strikes: The Black Death, Smallpox, AIDS*:

> A child orphaned by AIDS in Africa or a teenage prostitute fighting the virus in Thailand may not seem to have any connection to us. But in today's world, when one can fly to any continent within a matter of hours, they do.
>
> It took centuries for smallpox to reach the natives of North and South America from Europe. Things are very different now. Whether a new disease arises in central Africa, as AIDS apparently did, or in the deserts of the American Southwest, like the pulmonary hantavirus, it may be only a matter of days or weeks before it makes the journey from one continent to another.
>
> Given this undeniable fact, no new disease can remain a problem for only one group, nation, or even continent. Finding ways to treat and cure it soon becomes the concern of everyone on the planet.

Whichever tone seems appropriate, one element in the conclusion will always be the same, and it's as characteristic of the best nonfiction as it is of the finest fiction. This is the sense that in books, as in life, the story never really ends. Especially not in nonfiction aimed at an audience of young readers who, when they grow up, are bound to write new chapters of their own on every conceivable subject.

 Chapter Five

# Key Elements in Juvenile Fiction: The Idea, the Characters, and the Plot

A successful juvenile novel—like a successful nonfiction book—depends first of all on a good idea. Where do authors get the ideas for their stories? In the case of writers whose work I've edited, the ideas have seemed to come from a variety of sources, but few, if any, sprang from the authors' imaginations alone.

Many ideas emerged from real-life experiences. For example, Stella Pevsner heard one day of a divorced friend whose daughter discovered she was going to have her father's new wife—whom she hadn't yet met—as her seventh-grade math teacher. How would the girl react to the woman? How would the woman treat her? How would the girl's classmates interact with both of them? From this situation came Stella Pevsner's novel, *A Smart Kid Like You*, which was later made into the television movie titled, more explicitly, *Me and Dad's New Wife*.

Sometimes authors come across an idea for a novel while doing research for another project. Gloria Skurzynski, who writes nonfiction as well as fiction, got the idea for *Manwolf*, a historical novel for teenagers set in medieval Poland, when she was researching a medical nonfiction book and happened on the description of a rare skin disease that also causes the urine to turn red. People in the Middle Ages shunned victims of the disease and called them monsters, thus spawning the werewolf legend. Gloria imagined a boy who suffered from the disease; how would he cope with it and manage to survive? From these musings grew an unusual and powerful story.

Newspaper articles can also be an excellent source for fiction ideas. Like many other authors, Eve Bunting opens her morning paper each day with one eye cocked for a news story that might provide the basis for a novel. When she read a piece about a center in southern California devoted to the rehabilitation of injured birds, she immediately became intrigued. She arranged to visit the center, and when she saw that many teenagers worked there as volunteers, a thought occurred to her. What if one of the volunteers were a kid as much in need of rehabilitation as the birds he tended? That combination of situation and character gave Ms. Bunting the germ of her prize-winning novel, *One More Flight*.

But not all ideas lead to stories at once. Sometimes they come in fragments—a person from the author's past whom he keeps remembering and intends to work into a story someday; a dramatic situation the author wants to explore; a news story that fascinates him even though he doesn't know just how he would make use of it. If you get such ideas, don't ignore them or toss them out just because they're fragmentary. Instead, jot them down in your writing notebook or on a file card, or put them in a folder labeled "Ideas" in your computer. It may be six months or five years before one of them jells in your imagination, but whenever it happens you'll have the original idea on hand to refer to.

Looking more closely at the three book ideas just discussed, you can see that a common thread runs through them. Although the ideas themselves came from different sources—personal experience, historical research, a newspaper story—they triggered a similar response in their respective authors. It's a response that all writers of juvenile fiction can use as a measure of their own ideas. First, the ideas captured the authors' imaginations and made the authors want to explore them further. Next, they envisaged dramatic situations that embodied the ideas. And finally, they imagined a central character and wondered what that girl or boy would do if confronted by the particular situation. By then, the writers had already begun to transform their ideas into stories.

## Which comes first? The characters or the plot?

In shaping their stories, authors often ask which comes first, the characters or the plot. Ideally, the two should be blended closely from the start. But if you have to make a choice, you'll probably be on firmer ground if you begin with your central character.

You must know the character inside and out, psychologically as well as physically. And you must find effective ways to project your knowledge so that readers will recognize and identify strongly with the character from the moment he or she first appears in the story. These are not easy tasks. How can you best accomplish them?

Many successful fiction writers find it helpful to begin by putting the character—say he's a boy—in some sort of predicament. How he reacts and what he does will not only serve to get the story started, but will also give the reader a strong first impression of the character's temperament and personality.

The predicament can be a tense one, like the crisis that engulfs fourteen-year-old Danny at the beginning of Eve Bunting's suspense story, *Someone Is Hiding on Alcatraz Island*. Danny has turned in a gang member whom he saw mugging an old woman, and now the gang is out to get him. How will Danny escape their clutches? Or it can be a predicament involving social status and prestige, as in the opening situation in *Daphne's Book*, by Mary Downing Hahn. Jessica, the heroine of this novel, is unsure of her standing with the popular girls' clique, so she naturally becomes upset when

Daphne, the class outcast, is assigned as her partner in the sixth grade write-a-book project. Will she be ostracized by her "friends," Jessica wonders, if she accepts the assignment?

The predicament can even be amusing, as in Stella Pevsner's humorous story, *Me, My Goat, and My Sister's Wedding*. Doug, the hero, is secretly taking care of his best friend's pet goat while the friend is on vacation. One night the animal gets loose and frightens the neighbors when he peers into their living room window. How will Doug handle their complaints and still keep the goat hidden? (If you use a humorous situation like this in your story, don't forget one important thing: While a plight like Doug's may be funny to the reader, it usually creates a serious if not life-and-death problem for the character and should be treated accordingly. Avoid the temptation to snicker from the sidelines at the hero's dilemma; chances are you'll kill the humor if you do.)

Often, as your central character begins to take shape, a single physical or psychological characteristic will emerge as the dominant one in his personality makeup. In *Someone Is Hiding on Alcatraz Island*, Danny has to compensate for the fact that he's shorter and smaller than the gang members who are out to get him. In *Daphne's Book*, one of Jessica's chief traits is her insecurity in social situations, and it is this weakness that makes her even more reluctant to work with Daphne than she might have been otherwise. If you can find similarly dominant characteristics for your own fictional characters, you'll gain a head start in establishing their identities quickly and clearly in readers' minds.

## Reveal characters through action

Once you've introduced your central character and put him in a tight spot, how do you go about developing his personality—and those of the other characters—as the story progresses? *The first rule to remember is that a character should be revealed much more through action than description.*

Although you as author need to know at the outset what your characters look like and any distinctive mannerisms they may have, you can't expect readers to be interested automatically in lengthy accounts of their pasts or detailed descriptions of their physical features.

For example, it's usually not a good idea to stop the story to describe a character: "Felipe walked into the class-room. He had long black hair that fell at an angle over his forehead, and he was wearing a plaid shirt and faded jeans. The jeans were tucked into scuffed cowboy boots." Instead, try weaving the description of your character into the ongoing action of the scene: "Felipe walked into the classroom late and slouched down into his seat. It didn't look as if he'd combed his long black hair, which fell over his forehead as usual. When Miss Cho asked everybody to get ready to take some notes, Felipe fumbled into the pockets of his jeans for a pencil. As he did so, his scuffed cowboy boots made a scraping sound across the floor."

In shaping their characters, some authors refer to the notebooks in which they have jotted down brief descriptions of people who have caught their eye, or possible names for characters in future stories. Names are important in helping establish the background and even the personality of fiction-al characters. For example, readers would no doubt expect something funny from a character named Marvin Diddlebock, whereas they might guess that a character named Liz Ashford would turn out to be the pampered daughter of a well-to-do family.

Other authors clip pictures or ads from magazines or newspapers that show people who look like the characters they have in mind for a story, and use the pictures as models while they're writing. Still others make up long lists of their characters' preferences in food, clothing, movies, books, and music. They may also think of special turns of phrase or physical mannerisms and gestures the characters would be likely to use. For example, does the hero often duck his head when asked a hard question? Does his girlfriend have the habit of twisting a strand of her hair around a finger?

Many authors base their characters on real-life proto-types, sometimes people as close to them as their own children. The advantage of this approach is that it gives them a complete, in-the-round picture of a character without their having to construct the image from scratch. But there can also be serious disadvantages: The people in question may be embarrassed or even deeply hurt when they read the story and discover they're portrayed in it. To avoid such unpleas-antness, you should sufficiently alter the background and physical attributes of the characters so that the actual models won't recognize themselves. (Even then some friend or rela-tive may think he sees himself in one of your characters.)

You may also work from the inside out—like actors who follow Constantin Stanislavsky, a Russian actor, teacher, and director who created an approach to acting known as "the method." In order to prepare for a role, an actor using the Stanislavsky method would tap into emotional memory, drawing on experiences, instincts, and reactions from his or her past to build a character. Of course, all characters are, to some degree, reflections of their authors' personalities, espe-cially in stories that spring from incidents in an author's life and are largely autobiographical. However, there's a danger in relying on your own personality and feelings in book after book, for your characters may end up sounding and acting too much alike. It's usually wiser to make the characters a composite of different elements, including observation, imagination, and to some extent, real-life models, as well as your own emotions.

## First person or third person?

While you're getting your characters firmly in mind, you'll need to make an important decision before you actually begin to write your novel. That is the point of view from which you plan to tell the story: Will it be in the third person or the first person, and will the reader see the action from the vantage point of one character or several?

In the last 20 years or so, many authors of novels for young people—especially for teenagers—have chosen to write their stories in the first person. They feel it gives the stories a liveliness and immediacy that are more likely to catch and hold the attention of readers. This may be so, but a first-person viewpoint also imposes a great many restrictions on your story. Not only will you be limited to the events and actions that your viewpoint character observes or experiences, but you'll also have to work within the bounds of *his* intelligence and perception. The result is likely to be a story that's long on one-syllable words and slang, and short on the original turns of phrase and vivid descriptive passages that make for memorable fiction.

If an author is in doubt as to which point of view to choose—first person or third person—I always recommend third. It may be more difficult to manage because of the need to stand back and account for the actions and reactions of every character in the story, but it also allows for a great deal more flexibility. You'll be able to move in and out of the characters' thoughts as necessary, but at the same time be free to describe the shifting scenes from your own point of view as author.

Some authors of juvenile fiction have experimented with telling the story from multiple points of view. For example, if the novel is a teenage romance, the author may present the various stages of its development first from the girl's point of view and then from the boy's. Or in a novel of suspense, the viewpoint may alternate between a teenage robbery suspect attempting to elude capture and the police inspector who is determined to track him down. Shifting from one view to another like this can result in some amusing and dramatic contrasts, as in E. L. Konigsburg's Newbery Medal Book, *The View from Saturday*. But it can also end up being repetitive and confusing if not handled skillfully. The technique is usually more effective in novels for older readers who have experienced a variety of storytelling methods than in easy-reader and middle-grade stories directed toward youngsters who are still getting accustomed to the reading process. For the latter groups, I've generally found that a single viewpoint works better.

## Conflict: internal vs. external

Once you've settled on the point of view, you can go on to construct the overall plot of your novel. What exactly is a plot? Basically, it is the plan or blueprint for the story, the path it will follow from beginning to end. And it's generally triggered by the steps the hero takes to resolve the predicament he finds himself in at the outset.

Every textbook on writing states that in order to have a strong plot, you need conflict, and that conflict is generated when the hero is confronted by a powerful antagonist. That's true. But there are many different kinds of antagonists, both external and internal. In *Someone Is Hiding on Alcatraz Island* by Eve Bunting, for example, Danny is chased along the San Francisco waterfront in the first chapter by the gang members who are out to get him. The plot begins to take shape when Danny decides to try to elude his chief antagonist, the gang leader, by hopping aboard an excursion boat to Alcatraz. What he doesn't anticipate is that the gang will spot him and follow in the next boat, thus moving the plot forward. Here the conflict is largely external, although the hero, Danny, is also beset by internal doubts and fears stemming from his small stature.

In *Daphne's Book* by Mary Downing Hahn, on the other hand, the conflict is mainly internal, although the heroine, Jessica, uses external means to try to resolve it. First, she goes to her teacher and asks to be excused from working with Daphne on the write-a-book contest. When the teacher refuses, Jessica meets with Daphne but is cool and distant to the girl. By behaving in this way, Jessica hopes to signal the more popular girls that she really doesn't want to have anything to do with Daphne. Daphne surprises her, though, by turning out be an interesting person. Almost against her will, Jessica begins to care about Daphne, thereby heightening the conflict within herself and advancing the plot of the book.

The plot should be governed by the actions of the main characters, as in the two novels just discussed, and at the same time those actions should reveal new facets of the characters' personalities. How the secondary characters react to the events in the plot will serve to reveal their personalities, too. From all of these revelations will come that elusive quality that's a hallmark of all good fiction: depth.

## The importance of levels

Another way to give your novel depth is to make sure that you bring to the surface all the levels of meaning and significance that are inherent in the material. An excellent example of a novel that achieves this goal is Mary Downing Hahn's *Stepping on the Cracks*, winner of the Scott O'Dell Award for historical fiction.

At the outset, *Stepping on the Cracks* seems to be a story of friendship focused on two girls: shy Margaret and headstrong Elizabeth. But then the author begins to weave in additional levels. The first involves the time and place of the story: the last year of World War II in a small Maryland town. Hahn brings the period to life with carefully chosen details.

The war hasn't seriously affected Margaret and Elizabeth, although both girls have brothers serving in the armed forces. Their chief problem is Gordy, the class bully, who constantly torments them. Deciding to turn the tables on Gordy, the girls spy on his hideout in the woods and discover the boy's secret, which leads to the story's next level.

It seems Gordy is sheltering his brother Stu, a pacifist who has deserted from the army. Now the story becomes one of moral choices: What should Margaret and Elizabeth do—keep quiet about the deserter, whom they like as a person, or expose him to the authorities?

And what about Gordy? The girls find out he isn't as tough as they thought but lives in dread of his father, an abusive alcoholic. This adds another level to the boy's characterization.

At story's end, all plot threads are not tied up neatly. Stu turns himself in, Gordy and his family move away, and Margaret suffers the loss of her brother, killed in the Battle of the Bulge. Only her friendship with Elizabeth remains unchanged, a promise of hope for the future.

Several lessons can be learned about adding levels to your own stories from studying novels like *Stepping on the Cracks*. You might begin by asking yourself some basic questions when you're thinking about the plot for a new story and shaping its structure.

1. Does the main character have more than one issue to deal with, and do these issues bring out different aspects of the character? 2. Does the plot suggest the complexities of living—namely that one's actions can have both good and bad consequences? 3. Perhaps most important of all, is the theme an important one, like the exploration of patriotism and pacifism in *Stepping on the Cracks*? Without a meaningful theme, even a novel that's superior in other respects risks being thought trivial.

Although these questions may seem relevant only to serious novels, they can be applied with equal effect to humorous material. For all types of fiction, from stories designed purely to entertain to solemn studies of death and loss, will be more satisfying to the reader if they contain a number of different levels.

# Know where you're going

Authors often ask me if they should outline their novels before they begin to write. There's no hard-and-fast answer to that question: It all depends on the person. Some writers say they never write an outline for fear it will lessen their interest in the material and prove to be a deterrent. For instance, the late Jean Karl, the author of several science fiction novels for young people, once told me that she spent as long as a year thinking about her characters and what would happen to them in the course of the novel. Then, without writing any sort of outline, she simply sat down at her typewriter and let the first draft of the story pour out. "It tells itself to me as I go along," she said.

That approach may work for you, too, but most authors I've known feel more comfortable if they have some sort of outline on paper before starting their novels. The outline may be just a few brief notes for each chapter, or a detailed listing of all the twists and turns in the plot, complete with patches of dialogue and sometimes even complete scenes. Detailed outlines of the latter sort are probably most essential when you're writing a mystery and need to make sure that all the pieces of the plot fit together neatly. With other types of stories, there's a danger that too tight an outline will result in too schematic a manuscript. As editorial readers often say in their reports, "This novel has flashes of promise, but seems rigid and predictable. You can see the author's outline too clearly."

A better outlining method for most authors would probably be to start with the central character and sketch out a rough sequence of the major incidents in which he or she will be involved throughout the story. It's helpful to know at the outset where the chapter endings will come. And you'll definitely need to know, at least in general terms, how the story is going to end. Otherwise, how can you map out the best route to get to your destination?

Beginning authors who feel confused or unsure when they start to plot their novels often find it useful to take a juvenile book they admire and break it down into a chapter-by-chapter plot outline. By doing so, they can see in a bare-bones way how the author moved from one incident to another, where and how he wove in subplots and introduced important secondary characters, how he injected suspense and/or humor into the story, and how he built the narrative to a climax.

You may also find it helpful to trace the path of the central character's growth through a successful published novel. What was the character's situation at the beginning? How was his personality affected by the various events that occurred during the story? How is he different at the end from the way he was at the beginning? It's often from these differences, this pattern of growth, that the theme of a novel emerges—not imposed by the author from the outside, but arising naturally from the characters and situations in the story.

Exercises like these can help beginning writers to learn the storytelling techniques of successful authors and apply them to their own writing. They may also keep them from going off on tangents when they're planning their first novels, thus saving a great deal of time.

## Engage and intrigue

However you go about developing the plot of your novel, whether on paper or in your head, there are several basic elements that you should always bear in mind. They apply to all types of juvenile fiction—stories for beginning readers, longer books for the upper elementary audience, and novels for young adults.

1. Begin your story with an exciting incident. If you don't engage a reader's attention on the first page, or at the latest on the second, you'll never get it.

2. End each chapter with a development or twist that will make the reader eager to go on to the next. Whether the hero is in physical danger or brooding introspectively over a decision he must make, each chapter ending should grab the reader and leave him asking that classic question: "What's going to happen next?"

3. Be aware of pacing, and try to keep the chapters in your novel about the same length. You don't want your readers to become restless and start riffling the pages because a chapter goes on too long. On the other hand, you don't want them to feel cheated because another chapter seems too short. If a chapter turns out to be twice the length of the rest, maybe it should be divided at a dramatic point in the middle. If it's much shorter than the others—two or three manuscript pages instead of the usual eight or ten—maybe it can be added to the chapter that precedes it or to the one that follows.

4. Build the plot to a dramatic and satisfying climax. This doesn't mean that you have to tie up every loose end, answer every question that's been raised, or even bring the story to a happy ending. Life doesn't work that way, and critics and readers are likely to be skeptical if you violate their sense of reality. However, the major issues in the story should be resolved, readers should sense that the central character has grown in some way as a result of what he's experienced, and they should feel hopeful about his future.

In my opinion, a note of hope is a vital element in all types of juvenile fiction, for all age groups. While the best novelists writing for children don't deny that life has its problems and is often painful, they generally affirm that it's worth living. That's one of the qualities that distinguishes their books from many of the novels that are written and published for adults.

 Chapter Six

# Common Failings in Juvenile Fiction—and How to Correct Them

If a juvenile fiction author comes up with a good idea for a novel, one featuring strong characters and an unusual, involving plot, the result is almost sure to be a publishable manuscript, right? No, not always. In my years as a children's book editor, I've been distressed to read many novels by both first-time and experienced authors that fell short of their potential because the authors made one or more serious mistakes in storytelling. This chapter describes some of the most common of these failings, and suggests how they can be remedied.

1. *A dull beginning.* This problem often occurs because the chief character and his situation at the outset of the story aren't introduced in a compelling way. An author is likely to turn off readers, for example, if he devotes the first three pages of his manuscript simply to showing a teenage girl trying to decide what to wear on the first day of her sophomore year. He needs to have her dealing with a more serious issue. It doesn't have to be a life-and-death matter; suppose she's just completed a rigorous diet and is resisting the temptation to buy chocolate chip cookies in the school cafeteria? That should be enough to establish her personality and get the story moving.

2. *Too much exposition in the first chapter.* In an attempt to get the necessary exposition out of the way, many authors load their first chapters with lengthy passages detailing the

background of the story, and unlikely chunks of dialogue in which the characters explain themselves and their histories. After reading one such chapter, the editor I trained with early in my publishing career decreed: "All novels should begin with Chapter Two."

She may have been overstating the case, but she did have a point. I often have reason to remember her comment when I'm editing an exposition-heavy first chapter in a novel and suggest that the author simply cut it and weave the necessary background information into the subsequent chapters, in the form of brief flashbacks. In most instances, the suggestion results in a tighter, more involving story. It may work for you, too, if you are having problems with first-chapter exposition.

3. *Weak Transitions.* One of the hardest writing tasks for any author is to make smooth and interesting transitions between the scenes in his story. The transitions should give readers some clue as to when and where the next scenes are taking place so they won't be confused. But such clues should be worked in with a minimum of words in order to maintain the pace and drive of the story.

This can be tricky. Too many authors fall victim to what has been called "the door syndrome." In an attempt to make a transition absolutely clear, they feel they have to describe every move of the characters in great detail:

> After saying good-bye to Grandma, Alyssa went over to the front door and slowly turned the handle. As the door swung open, she stepped through it and closed it gently behind her. Then she walked down the drive to the sidewalk and hurried along it to Trazana's house where she had been invited for lunch.

Do we really need to know how Alyssa opened and

closed the door? Wouldn't the transition work just as well— and get us more quickly to the next scene—if it simply read:

> After saying good-bye to Grandma, Alyssa hurried over to Trazana's house where she had been invited for lunch.

That's probably how I would edit the transition if I found it in a manuscript. You should keep an eye out for similar cases of "the door syndrome" in your next novel and try to correct them before you send the manuscript to a publisher.

If you find it hard to solve the problem simply by rewriting the text, perhaps you can try another scene-shifting technique that's worked well for many authors: the use of a two- or-three-line blank space between paragraphs to denote the passing of time, or a change of locale, or both. I liken this technique to a film director cutting abruptly from one scene to another in a movie. It can help to give a novel a faster pace, and is especially effective in stories of suspense where the author may need to switch quickly from the hero, who is caught in a tight spot, to his friends, who are trying to make contact with him.

But guard against relying too heavily on space breaks. If you overuse them, your writing is likely to seem choppy and disjointed. You'll probably be better off if you solve most of your transition problems in the writing itself and employ space breaks only when you want to achieve a special effect.

4. *Vary the mood.* Rembrandt, Shakespeare, and other great artists and writers knew something that too many juvenile novelists forget: namely, that light stands out much more vividly if it's contrasted with shadow, and vice versa. If you're writing a story centered on drugs, child abuse, teenage suicide, or some other serious problem, it's a mistake to maintain an unremittingly grim mood. Silly things can be said and done in the midst of tragic events, and often

are. If you inject bits of humor into your story, you'll not only vary the mood, but in all likelihood will present a more convincing and true-to-life picture.

On the other hand, if you're writing a humorous story don't be afraid to weave some serious undertones into it. The class clown may not think life is so funny when he's by himself; the joke that breaks up everyone in the fifth grade may be extremely hurtful to the person at whom it's directed. If you show both sides of such situations, you'll amuse your readers while giving them something to think about, too.

5. *Thin characterizations.* This is one of the most frequent—and most frustrating—mistakes that authors make in fiction manuscripts. Their heroes are too heroic, the villains are too villainous, and as a result their stories seem unbelievable. To avoid such failures, it's a good idea when you're planning your story and shaping the characterizations to think of a few weaknesses that will lend credibility to your hero. For example, Tom may be a star athlete who responds immediately to any physical demand made on him. But he may also have a tendency to act rashly before he's thought through a problem. As readers see him struggling to overcome this weakness, Tom will seem more human—and more genuinely heroic. And so will your protagonists, if you give them similar feelings to grapple with.

The reverse is true of villains. In too many stories, they have no redeeming features whatsoever and consequently it's hard to take them seriously. How many people do we know in life who are totally bad? The meanest bully may love his grandmother; the most manipulative girl in seventh grade may be a gifted artist. So give your villains a few positive qualities; chances are they'll be much more convincing to readers if you do.

Remember, too, that people who behave in evil ways are often blind to the true nature of their actions. In their eyes, they aren't doing anything wrong. That only makes them— and fictional characters like them—all the more frightening.

6. *Holes in the plot.* Our daily lives are filled with coincidences and chance meetings, but we don't like to encounter them in the plots of novels. Sid Fleischman, the well-known author of many comic stories for young readers including his Newbery Medal winner, *The Whipping Boy*, offers writers some excellent advice on how to handle this problem: If there's a hole in your plot that you can't get rid of, don't try to hide it from readers. Instead, call attention to it. For example, it's better to have a character say, "I know it's hard to believe, but I ran into so-and-so on the street today" than to have your readers think the happening is hard to believe.

7. *Problems with dialogue.* The misuse of dialogue is responsible for many failings in juvenile novels of all types. Here are some examples that I often see in the first drafts of novels and try to help the authors correct through revision.

(a) *Show, don't tell.* A key to overcoming this problem lies in the classic bit of advice that writing teachers have been imparting to their students for generations: "Show, don't tell." In line with this precept, it's usually a good idea to dramatize a scene, however brief, through dialogue and action rather than sum it up in a description. The descriptive approach too often results in an undesirable flatness, as in the sample scene that follows:

> After I got permission from Mrs. DiCenza to go to the guidance counselor's office, I left the classroom and walked down the hall to the spot where I had told my friend Tyrone I'd meet him. I was standing there, trying to look as if I belonged, when who should come along but Mrs. DiCenza.
> She got mad when she saw me and asked some questions. I tried to explain what I was doing there, but she didn't really listen to me.

Instead, she told me I'd have to go with her to the principal's office.

After reading such a passage, I'd probably comment in the margin, "This needs some dialogue to give it life. What questions does Mrs. DiCenza ask the boy? How does he try to explain why he's in the hall?" And here's how the author, in an attempt to show rather than tell, might revise the scene:

> A few minutes later I was standing in the hall, trying to look as if I belonged there, when who should come along but Mrs. DiCenza.
> She frowned when she saw me. "What are you doing here, Chris? I thought you told me you had an appointment with the guidance counselor."
> "Well, I do—I mean, I did," I tried to explain. "But you see my friend Tyrone's in trouble, and I said I'd meet him here before next period . . ."
> Mrs. DiCenza interrupted before I could finish. "It looks as if Tyrone's not the only one who's in trouble," she said. "I think you'd better come along with me to the principal's office, Chris."

(b) *Too much unbroken dialogue.* Sometimes, instead of failing to dramatize a scene through dialogue, authors make the opposite mistake. They rely so heavily on dialogue alone that the reader may become confused and forget who's speaking. That's what occurs, as you'll see, in this sample exchange between two girls:

> "Where would you like to go later?"
> "I don't know. Maybe a movie?"
> "Why not? They say that new picture about aliens from another galaxy is really exciting."

> "I don't like all that science fiction stuff. I'd rather see the new Julia Roberts picture. The reviewer on Channel 7 said it was terrific."
>
> "Oh, not Julia Roberts. She's always the same."

The dialogue per se isn't what's wrong with that scene. What it lacks is a sense of context. This can often be corrected by weaving in some narrative sentences. Such sentences will not only serve to identify the speakers, but they can also be used to deepen the characterization and advance the plot.

Here's a revision of the scene, employing the exact same dialogue, but it shows how much more texture a few descriptive sentences can bring to it:

> "Where would you like to go later?" I asked.
>
> "I don't know," said Sandra. "Maybe a movie?"
>
> That wasn't a bad idea. I'd overheard Bruce and Jerry talking about going to the sci-fi movie at the mall tonight. Maybe we'd run into them and. . . . "Why not?" I said. "They say that new picture about aliens from another galaxy is really exciting."
>
> "I don't like all that science fiction stuff," Sandra said. "I'd rather see the new Julia Roberts picture. The reviewer on Channel 7 said it was terrific."
>
> I was pretty sure none of the guys would go to *that* picture.
>
> "Oh, not Julia Roberts," I said. "She's always the same."

Notice that in the second version of the scene the author avoided unusual verbs and used no adverbs. Too many writers feel they need to enliven their dialogue by accompanying it with a different verb every time, and following each verb with an adverb. When I read a manuscript page filled with such expressions as "he muttered darkly," "she snarled nastily," "he whispered shakily," and "she cried happily," my immediate impulse is to edit them all down to a simple "he said" and "she said." The dialogue, if it's lively and appropriate, will let the reader know how the character is saying it, and no adverb will be necessary.

(c) *Dialogue that's too "trendy."* Children and teenagers constantly latch onto new expressions and make them their own. What's "swell" for one generation is "neato" for the next and "awesome" for the one after that. Authors want to be *au courant,* but with the pace of cultural change seeming to accelerate each year, they run the risk of sounding dated if they incorporate such expressions in the dialogue of their novels. Even expressions that are right up-to-the-minute when the manuscript is written may be out of date or unknown to readers by the time the book is published two years later.

I often recall what the well-known novelist for young adults, M. E. Kerr, replied when asked how she managed to keep the dialogue in her stories up-to-date: "I don't try," she said. "I do my best to avoid slang and jargon and rely on simple, basic words to express my characters' feelings."

As an editor, I also question the overuse of contemporary references and suggest that authors find other ways to convey their characters' preferences in movies and music. Most hardcover juvenile novels—unlike most adult novels—stay in print for at least three years, and often many more. So why fill them with references to rock groups and TV stars who may be long forgotten when the books are still finding readers?

8. *Weak entrances and exits.* Many fiction manuscripts are seriously weakened because the authors fail to provide their characters with effective entrances into key scenes and strong exits out of them. The first entrance of a main character in the story is especially important. Skillfully handled, it can establish

the personality of the character in a few swift strokes. If the moment is lost, though, it may require several pages of dialogue and description to convey what a dramatic entrance would have accomplished in a couple of paragraphs.

Suppose, for example, that your heroine is a likable but clumsy girl who's invariably late and always seems to trip over her own feet. In the first draft of the story you may pass too quickly over her first entrance, as in the excerpt that follows:

> Amanda walked into the kitchen around ten on that Saturday morning, her skates dangling over one shoulder. "Hi, Mom," she said. "Sorry I'm late. I just couldn't seem to get myself together."
>
> "I understand, dear," Mrs. Romano said, "but I'm afraid you'll have to make your own breakfast."

There's nothing glaringly wrong with that exchange; it just isn't very interesting. And it certainly doesn't make use of Amanda's entrance to give the reader a vivid first impression of her. In an editorial note, I might ask the author if Amanda's mother is exasperated when Amanda is late for breakfast again. Does she call up to her? And what about Amanda? Does she have any problems on the stairs before we see her? After pondering these questions, here's how the author might rework the scene:

> Mrs. Romano strode over to the archway and called upstairs. "Amanda, where are you? It's nearly ten!"
>
> "Be there in a sec, Mom," Amanda called back. "I couldn't find my skates and then—" Suddenly there was a crash in the upstairs hall followed by the sound of something rolling down the steps.

"Oh, oh, one of them got away."

As Mrs. Romano watched, hands on hips, a roller skate clattered to a halt on the landing with Amanda right behind it. The girl's hair was a mass of tangled red curls and the tail of her blouse dangled below her sweater.

"Got you!" Amanda said as she reached down to pick up the wayward skate. But in retrieving it she lost her grip on the other one. The second skate banged down the short flight of steps to the hall and was headed across it when Mrs. Romano stopped it with her toe.

A bright red blush spread across Amanda's face. "Sorry, Mom," she said.

Mrs. Romano had to smile. "Oh, Amanda, what are we going to do about you?"

In that revision, we get a much sharper picture of Amanda, and it's achieved through a lively, amusing scene that advances the story's action. Ideally, that's what every first entrance should do.

## Fleshing out an exit

Exits can be as difficult to manage as entrances, and often more so. Sometimes I sense that authors shy away from making the most of a character's exit for fear of seeming melodramatic. But I'd much rather see an author risk a little melodrama than throw away the possibility for a strong exit, as happens in the following exchange between a father and son:

"I don't want to hear any more about it," Mr. Andrews said. "You're grounded for two weeks, Ben, and that's that."

"All right," Ben said. He left the living room and went up the stairs to his room.

That exit is so understated that it's virtually no exit at all. What is Ben feeling? we wonder. Is he angry, bitter, resigned? How does he leave the room—slowly, quickly? How does he go up the stairs? Dragging his heels, hoping his father will call him back? Or in a run, wanting to get away from the man as soon as possible? In responding to those questions, the author might come up with this revision:

> "I don't want to hear any more about it," Mr. Andrews said. "You're grounded for two weeks, Ben, and that's that." He turned away then, and went to the bar to pour himself a fresh drink.
>
> "All right," Ben muttered under his breath, so softly that he doubted if Dad heard. *Who cares?* he thought to himself. *Dad never hears anything I say anyway.*
>
> With a last glance at his father's back, Ben left the room and started up the stairs. He took them one at a time, giving his father a chance to call him back if he wanted to. But he didn't; Ben hadn't really expected that he would.
>
> When he reached the door to his room, Ben had a momentary impulse to slam it behind him, then decided against it. Instead he closed the door so gently that he could barely hear the latch click into place.

Fleshing out an exit in this fashion can accomplish several things at once. Here, as Ben climbs the stairs to his room the reader gains an insight into the boy's emotions and sees how he reacts to a crisis. However, authors are sometimes reluctant to undertake such revisions. They worry that if they do, their manuscripts will get too long and seem overwritten. They should keep in mind one of the basic principles of editing—namely, that it is always easier to make cuts in a scene that goes too far than to build up a scene that doesn't go far enough.

9. *Mid-book sags.* Sometimes, as I begin to read a new fiction manuscript by one of our regular authors, a smile comes over my face. The characters and situation are interesting, the plot is moving forward at a rapid clip, dialogue and description are in just the right balance. Then I turn the page and my smile fades, for I realize that the story has suddenly sagged. It's only temporary, I hope, and I keep on reading. But now I have my editorial pencil out, ready to jot down suggestions that may help the author get the story back on track.

When I analyze the problem, I usually find that the cause of the sag is a scene or character that doesn't advance the plot. Often an author wants to take the characters to a particular locale—say an amusement park or a county fair—because the author thinks it will add color to the story; instead, it merely slows it down. Or perhaps an author will introduce a character who seemed necessary at outline stage, but who has no real part to play as the story takes shape on paper.

The latter was the cause of a serious mid-book sag in the first draft of Stella Pevsner's novel, *Cute Is a Four-Letter Word.* The heroine, Clara, lived with her divorced mother near Chicago, and the entire action of the novel took place there except for one chapter when Clara visited her father, an advertising executive in New York City. He took her sightseeing and they had several warm conversations in which they admitted that they missed each other. But none of this seemed to have any bearing on the plot of the story, which picked up only after Clara returned to Chicago.

I pointed out this sag to the author in my editorial letter; she thought about the problem for a few days, and then she called me with a possible solution. "Why don't I just kill off Dad?" she said. "I don't think I need him in the story." I agreed, and in the published book Clara's father has been dead for several years, and she makes no trip to New York.

If you hit a similar mid-book sag in one of your own novels, it's usually a good idea to go back to the original notes or outline and ask yourself some hard questions. Does every episode and character help to move the story toward its conclusion, or are some of them extraneous? If your answer to the latter half of that question is "yes," then drastic surgery may be called for, as was the case in *Cute Is a Four-Letter Word*. Such surgery can be painful for you to perform because you may lose a favorite character or plot twist in the process. But it'll probably result in a tighter manuscript—one that will hold your readers' attention to the end.

10. *An unsatisfying ending.* Just as the beginning of a novel should draw readers swiftly and surely into the story, so the ending should send them away satisfied and elated. I have my own test for a successful ending: Does it send tingles down my spine? In far too many instances I'm disappointed, and—sensing that young readers will be also—I try to get at the reason the ending failed to move me so that I can help the author come up with a better alternative.

Often I find that the author has spent all of his or her energy in building the novel to a strong climax and has then cut off the denouement too abruptly. That's what happened in the first draft of Mary Downing Hahn's *Daphne's Book*. After Jessica, the heroine, learned that her friend Daphne and her little sister Hope were living with their senile grandmother and trying to keep the woman's condition a secret, Jessica promised not to tell her mother or anyone else about their problem. But when the grandmother's condition worsened and Jessica feared what she might do to Daphne and Hope, Jessica broke her promise. In the climax, she told her mother about the situation, and her mother in turn informed a social worker. The grandmother was taken to a hospital where she soon died, and only much later did Jessica learn, via a letter from Daphne, that she and Hope were now living with a cousin in Maine.

From the climax on, this ending was a letdown. What was needed was more than just a letter from Daphne; readers would want to see the girls together one more time. So the author added a powerful new scene in which Jessica visits Daphne and Hope at Roseland, the children's home where they're staying until their cousin can come for them. At the beginning of the scene, Daphne is still angry with Jessica for having betrayed her and her grandmother to the authorities. Jessica manages to explain herself, however, and by scene's end the girls have reached a bittersweet understanding. Their friendship is as strong as ever, but they know they'll soon be parted, perhaps forever. Here's how the novel ended now:

> "Good-bye, Jessica." Daphne released my hand and turned toward Roseland. "Did you really mean what you said?" she asked suddenly, her face swinging toward me in the dusk.
>
> I nodded, knowing immediately what she meant. "Yes, you're the best friend I've ever had."
>
> "You, too," she said. Then she was gone, running toward the glowing windows of Roseland with Hope behind her, looking back and waving.

When I came to those final paragraphs in the revised manuscript, my spine was really tingling. Apparently they had the same effect on other readers, for reviewer after reviewer commented on the book's strong ending, and the author received numerous letters from young readers saying it had made them cry.

What lesson can be learned from this? Simply that readers young and old like nothing better than to have a good cry—or laugh—when they finish a book. So don't be afraid to pull out all the stops and write the ending of your novel as fully and emotionally as you can. If you go too far, your editor will bring you back to earth. But if you hit the right notes, chances are you'll arrive at an ending that your readers will remember for years to come.

 Chapter Seven

# The Five Ages of Juvenile Fiction

The basics of idea, characterization, and plot, of skillful dialogue, humor, and strong conclusions, are common to all types of juvenile fiction. However, each age group, from easy stories for beginning readers to young adult novels, has its own specific requirements. This chapter will explore the needs of each group in turn, starting with stories aimed at children of six to nine.

## Easy readers

Easy reading stories are designed for children in the early elementary grades who have graduated from picture books but aren't quite ready to tackle full-length novels. The pattern for all future easy readers was set by Harper & Row in 1957, when the firm published the first title in its "I Can Read" series, *Little Bear* by Else Holmelund Minarik, with illustrations by Maurice Sendak. Its format resembled a regular children's novel, but the text was set in larger type than usual and the book was only 64 pages long.

By the 1970s, Harper had hundreds of "I Can Read" titles in print, and a half dozen or so other publishers had jumped on the easy-to-read bandwagon with their own series. The market for easy readers became glutted, and in recent years many series have been dropped. But Harper (now known as HarperCollins) and several other houses continue to publish them, and children in first and second grade still turn to easy readers when they're looking for "a real book."

If you think you'd like to write an easy reader, it's important to keep several basic rules in mind. First, the format of an easy reader is more rigid than that of any other type of juvenile fiction. As in *Little Bear*, there are almost always a certain number of characters in each line of type, and a certain number of lines per page. If the story is divided into chapters, there may be a desired number of text lines per chapter, and most easy-reading series have a standard length for the manuscript as a whole. Some publishers also require authors of easy readers to work from a limited list of simple words prepared by a reading expert.

Before you begin to plan your easy-reading story, let alone write it, you should obtain the particular specifications of one or more publishers of easy readers. You should also study some of the easy-reading titles you admire to see how the authors structured their stories.

Watch out, though; in mastering the *form* of the easy-reading book, too many authors neglect the *content*. They forget that no youngster will stick with a book just because it's easy. It has to be interesting, funny, or exciting—like any other type of fiction—if it's going to capture and hold the reader's attention. So, when you're developing your easy-to-read story, don't think it has to be a gentle, whimsical tale of animal friends or a mild account of a second-grade tiff. A plethora of those were published at the height of the easy-reading vogue and probably contributed to its decline.

Concentrate instead on the same basics of idea, characters, and plot as you would for a longer novel. Don't rule out any type of story: mysteries, historical stories, and science fiction tales have all appeared in an easy-reading format, along with home-and-school stories and animal fantasies. And remember that the use of simple words and short sentences doesn't mean the writing style has to be choppy or dull. The best easy-reading stories, like Arnold Lobel's books about Frog and Toad, achieve a kind of poetry through the careful choice of words linked in a flowing, rhythmic manner. That's the effect you should aim for in your own stories.

## Chapter books

The next step up from easy readers is a type of story that has become known in recent years as a chapter book. These are stories written in short chapters and directed toward seven-to-ten-year-olds. Chapter books have also been called "chewy stories," meaning ones that youngsters who have gone beyond easy readers, but aren't quite ready for full-length novels, can really get their teeth into.

While the name chapter book may be new, the form is not. Maud Hart Lovelace, Carolyn Haywood, Beverly Cleary, and others were writing skillful stories in chapters for the seven-to-ten age group as far back as the 1940s, and there are earlier examples dating to the early years of the twentieth century. What is new is the greater emphasis publishers are putting on the category, and the wider range of opportunities it offers to authors.

Recent examples are the books by H. B. Homzie and Matt Phillips such as *Who Let the Dogs Out?* and *The Baby-Sitters Wore Diapers* and Mary Pope Osborne's Magic Tree House series.

Chapter books are almost always divided into chapters of five to seven manuscript pages, and the overall manuscript may run anywhere from 30 to 100 pages, depending on the complexity of the story. Unlike easy readers, chapter books do not have to be written to any exact limitations in terms of characters per line of text or a controlled vocabulary. But most of them have a tighter focus than novels for older children.

The cast of characters is generally small, and the action takes place within a fairly short time span. In this regard, chapter books resemble long short stories or novellas more than full-length novels. Consequently, when you're thinking of writing a chapter book, you should avoid a complicated plot with subplots and look for an idea that can be expressed through a single dramatic (or comic) situation.

Chapter books, like easy readers, run the entire fictional gamut from realistic stories such as Jane Resh Thomas's moving account of a farm boy and his fearful pup, *The Comeback Dog*, to Stephen Manes's broad farce, *Be a Perfect Person in Just Three Days*. Although the manuscripts are short, multi-leveled relationships can still be explored, as in Carla Stevens's *Anna, Grandpa, and the Big Storm*, and strong feelings expressed, as in Sue Alexander's *Lila on the Landing*. The genre also embraces historical fiction, the most notable example of which is undoubtedly Patricia MacLachlan's Newbery Medal-winning story of two frontier children and their father's mail-order bride, *Sarah, Plain and Tall*.

The chapter book is no longer limited to seven-to-ten-year-olds, either. In recent years, as the trend in children's fiction has been toward shorter manuscripts, many authors of novels for upper-elementary-grade readers and even some for young adults have employed the small cast and close focus of the chapter book in their more mature books. So if you have an idea for a small scale work, don't dismiss it out of hand as suitable only for short story treatment. Examine it carefully to see if it might be shaped into a chapter book.

## Middle-grade fiction

The phrase "middle-grade fiction" has nothing to do with its quality. It refers to fiction written for children in the middle elementary grades—probably the largest single audience for children's book writers. Why is this so? Because children eight to twelve are old enough to enjoy reading and can handle full-length novels, but are still young enough to want books written especially for them. After they reach the age of twelve or so, many readers move on to young adult fiction, or to adult books.

Fiction aimed at the middle-grade group is dominated by contemporary home-and-school stories, although publishers' catalogues also include a considerable number of mystery, fantasy, and historical novels for eight-to-twelve-year-olds. The requirements for the latter three categories will be taken up in the next chapter; as for stories with home and school settings, they usually rely more on dialogue than on description and move at a fairly rapid clip. In editing them, I often suggest that authors divide longer paragraphs in two for ease of reading and a faster pace. Most chapters in middle-grade novels run to 10 or 12 manuscript pages, and few manuscripts are more than 150 pages long.

Following the longstanding precept that youngsters like to read about children who are a little older than themselves, most of the protagonists in middle-grade fiction are 12 or 13. The problems confronting these heroes and heroines cover a broad spectrum. They range from worries about a seventh-grade prom, as in Eve Bunting's *Janet Hamm Needs a Date for the Dance*, to coping emotionally with the death of a best friend, as in Katherine Paterson's Newbery Medal-winning *Bridge to Terabithia*.

Some authors, when planning a novel for middle-grade readers, decide to extend their idea and plot into a whole series of stories about the central character or characters. This is understandable, given the popularity of such long-standing series stars as Nancy Drew and the Hardy Boys, and more recent characters like Beverly Cleary's Ramona, Lois Lowry's Anastasia Krupnik, and the preteen cast of Ann Martin's phenomenally successful Baby-Sitters' Club series. But it usually proves to be a risky practice. In most cases, authors would be well advised to wait until young readers respond strongly to a character before writing more stories about him or her. Meanwhile, they can concentrate their energies on making the first story about that character as saleable as possible.

Lively, well-written novels for upper elementary age readers have been in demand ever since publishers began to issue separate lists of children's books in the early 1920s. If you have a feeling for this age group and can think of story ideas that would appeal to it, you stand a very good chance of finding a publisher for your manuscript—and an enthusiastic audience of young readers.

## Transitional fiction

Between middle-grade fiction and young adult fiction is a more amorphous category that I call "transitional fiction." This category embraces stories that help readers between the ages of 10 and 14 to make the transition from younger to more mature story material.

Titles play an important role in attracting the attention of this age group, and authors have come up with some catchy ones in the last couple of decades. Among those that stick in the memory are E. L. Konigsburg's *From the Mixed-Up Files of Mrs. Basil E. Frankweiler*, John Donovan's *I'll Get There, It Better Be Worth the Trip*, and Paula Danziger's *The Cat Ate My Gymsuit*. Be careful, though, not to push a title idea too far and end up with one that seems forced rather than clever.

As with middle-grade fiction, most transitional novels move along at quite a rapid pace in chapters of twelve or so manuscript pages, with the total length of the book rarely exceeding 200 pages. The subjects treated in transitional novels are similar to those in middle-grade fiction, and the time periods covered range from the ancient past to the far future. However, starting in the 1960s and continuing into the early 1980s, the field often seemed to be dominated by the "problem novel."

Judy Blume pioneered the problem genre and aroused

controversy with such titles as *Are You There, God? It's Me, Margaret*, which touched on Margaret's confusion about adolescence and religion, and *Then Again, Maybe I Won't*, which confronted a boy's problems with the advent of puberty. Other authors, including Norma Klein, Richard Peck, John Donovan, and R. R. Knudson followed in Judy Blume's wake with problem stories of their own. By the 1970s there was virtually no topic, from drug addiction to child abuse to homosexuality, that hadn't been explored in at least one transitional novel for young teens.

With the 1980s came an inevitable counter-reaction. Conservative groups launched campaigns to have books they considered "indecent and immoral" removed from school and public libraries, and many of the titles they attacked were teenage problem novels. At the same time, young readers themselves, reflecting the mood of the country, began to lose interest in problem stories and expressed a preference for light, romantic fiction. Authors and publishers responded with series after series of romance novels, most of which appeared in a paperback format.

Following in their wake, series of horror stories, such as Goosebumps and Fear Street by R. L. Stine and thrillers by Christopher Pike, have attracted a large audience of young teens. These series were no doubt inspired by the popularity of Stephen King's and Dean Koontz's adult horror novels among teenage readers.

In light of such swings in audience reaction, I usually advise authors who approach me with an idea for a problem novel to put the characters and plot, not the problem, in first place. The day when any subject, in and of itself, was enough to generate reader interest is long over. If the characters in a novel aren't convincing and the plot compelling, hardcover editors aren't likely to give the manuscript serious consideration, no matter how timely and urgent a problem it explores.

The same is true of teenage romance novels: They have to contain more than just romance in order to justify the high price of a hardcover book. As for paperback publication, a certain "Hollywoodization" seems to have occurred in the romance field in recent years. More and more paperback editors appear to be relying on series stories which, like the scripts for a television series, are generally written on assignment by established professionals. Consequently, it's become more difficult for a newcomer to break into the paperback romance field.

Nor are romances as easy to write as many authors think. To bring one off successfully, you must care as passionately as your heroine about clothes, hair, the state of her complexion, and whether or not the handsome new boy in school will look her way. In this connection, I'm reminded of a conversation I once had with Jane Claypool Miner, author of many popular teenage romances. When I asked her how she achieved the enthusiastic tone of her books, she said, "I was a very romantic teenager myself—I loved to go shopping and try out new make-up and hair styles. In fact, I still do. So I just draw on all that when I'm creating my characters, and I guess it must get across to my readers." I have a hunch that this kind of empathy is a prerequisite for all writers of romance novels.

Horror stories present a different set of problems for the writer. How can one achieve the necessary chills and suspense without resorting to the mindless bloodletting found in so many contemporary movies and television programs?

One way is to describe a violent act by implication rather than spell out every gory detail. Alfred Hitchcock made skillful use of this technique in many of his films. If he was telling the story of an axe-murderer, he could fill the viewer with a sense of dread and shock without ever showing the axe falling or blood flowing.

Above all, don't surrender your own values and inherent

good taste to what you may perceive to be the demands of the marketplace. Even if you're writing a horror novel to the specifications of a teen paperback series, what's to prevent you from writing it as well as you are able and developing the characters in depth? No doubt your editor will appreciate the smooth, satisfying way you've managed to tell your story. So will your readers, although they may not articulate it. And you can take an honest pride in your work instead of feeling cynical about it.

## Fiction for young adults

No one has ever been able to agree on an exact definition of the young adult audience. Some will tell you it begins with kids as young as 10 or 11, and extends upward to teenagers of 16 or 17. Those who hold a more traditional view say the audience is limited to teenage readers between the ages of 14 and 18. Others—and I count myself among them—think young adult novels provide teenage readers with a sort of bridge between children's and adult fiction. Some readers are ready to cross that bridge when they're 11 or 12. Others don't cross it until they're 13 or 14 or even older.

Young adult fiction came into its own in the 1950s, 1960s, and 1970s with the publication of such enduring classics as Paul Zindel's *The Pigman* and Robert Cormier's *The Chocolate War*. It suffered a decline in the 1980s, but bounced back strongly in the late 1990s. The resurgence was fueled by a broadening of the potential audience, coupled with a willingness on the part of writers and publishers to tackle difficult subject matter and present it in innovative ways. Recognizing the new vitality in the field, the American Library Association in 2000 established the Michael L. Printz Award for young adult literature, named in honor of a pioneer young adult librarian in Kansas.

Early Printz Award winners and Honor Books suggest the range—and the sometimes controversial nature—of young adult fiction. Walter Dean Myers's *Monster* tells the story of 16-year-old Steve, who has been arrested and charged with the murder of a Korean shopkeeper. While in jail, Steve writes a screenplay about the incident, interspersed with entries from the journal he keeps. This unique form of storytelling keeps readers guessing and makes them ask, "Is Steve guilty—or is he innocent?"

Two other winners explore other aspects of teenage life. In Ellen Wittlinger's *Hard Love*, the leading characters, John and Marisol, have a lot in common. Both are concerned about the issue of trust, both have problem parents, and both, as it turns out, are attracted to girls. John and Marisol discuss their problems quite freely, but Melinda, the heroine of Laurie Halse Anderson's *Speak*, remains frustratingly silent for much of the novel. Only gradually does she gain the courage to reveal that she has been sexually assaulted—and to name the attacker.

Obviously these books and others like them are a far cry from the typical young adult novel of old, whose big moment occurred when the hero gave the heroine her first kiss after bringing her home from the Senior Prom. Editors often say what they're looking for today are "edgy" stories, which translates into manuscripts that tackle difficult or unusual subject matter and treat it in a no-holds-barred way.

But edgy doesn't necessarily mean shocking. A novel can deal with more conventional subject matter—the rapture of first love, the loss of a best friend, the death of a parent—and still seem edgy if the characters are sharply observed and the writing has a distinctive tone that immediately grabs the reader's attention. Humorous novels can have an edge, too, as can novels written for the religious market.

Whether the story material breaks new ground or brings fresh insights to familiar situations, certain traits distinguish most young adult novels from their adult counterparts. They're usually shorter, no more than 200 manuscript pages, and the central character is almost always a teenager. If the story includes sex scenes, they're generally less graphic than those in an adult novel. Profanity in dialogue is used sparingly if at all. And the endings of most young adult novels, like the endings of stories for younger children, are usually realistic but hopeful.

Some writers steer completely clear of the young adult field, saying they have no idea what teenage life is like today. Or else they feel uncomfortable with the relaxation of taboos in terms of subject matter. But for those of you who feel you do have a finger on the adolescent pulse, the market for young adult fiction has rarely been as strong as it is now.

 Chapter Eight

# Different Types of Fiction

W ithin each age group, from the "easy reading" category to novels for young adults, several different types of fiction frequently appear. The most common of these types are mysteries; historical fiction; multicultural stories; fantasies, including science fiction; and a more recent but fast-growing category: graphic novels. Let's look now at some of the special requirements for each type, starting with mysteries.

## Mystery stories

Back in the early 1960s, many juvenile mysteries still fell into what some critics called the "Who buried the family treasure in the backyard?" category. A brother and sister, often named Johnny and Janie, visited Great Aunt Louisa's farm for the summer, and while there discovered a priceless heirloom that an ancestor had buried in the back garden for safekeeping during the Civil War.

Mystery stories like this were immensely popular in the 1940s and 1950s, and some are still being submitted for possible publication. Few are accepted, however, since readers now want their mysteries to have a contemporary feel. For younger children, that often means stories about a bunch of bright, perky kids who solve a neighborhood mystery. The setting is usually suburban—after all, how many children today have a Great Aunt Louisa who lives on a farm?—and the tone is light and laced with humor. Entertaining examples of this type of mystery, for children seven to ten or so, have been written by Susan Meyers, Dorothy Haas, and E. W. Hildick.

Successful mysteries for middle-grade readers have a sharper edge than their counterparts in the past and often center on a contemporary problem such as drugs or shoplifting. A good example of this trend is Barbara Holland's suspense story about a kidnapping, *Prisoners at the Kitchen Table*, in which a wealthy young girl and her friend, a cautious boy, are held for ransom by a husband-and-wife team and must find a way to escape from their captors. Similar stories of suspense, such as those written by Joan Lowery Nixon and Lois Duncan, are popular with readers 10 and up.

## The plot thickens

In *plotting* a mystery for any age group, you should keep in mind certain basic questions that will have to be answered during the course of the story:

1. What really happened? You'll need to know this before you start writing so that you can place clues logically and dramatically along the way.

2. Who is the detective, and why does he or she want to solve the mystery? What's at stake? Even in a lighthearted mystery for younger readers, the stake should be something important—at least to the central character. Finding a missing glove probably wouldn't be enough to sustain a story, but finding a missing bicycle might be.

3. What's the detective's plan of action for solving the mystery? What active steps does he or she take? From these the plot will naturally grow.

4. What's the opposition? Who's out to stop the central character from solving the mystery—and why? The conflict in the story will spring from your answers to these questions.

5. What's the time limit? If the central character has only

a few days or a week to solve the mystery, tension will be heightened. This time limit doesn't have to involve anything as dramatic as a bomb going off. In Dorothy Haas's *To Catch a Crook*, the limit is just a deadline for a Career Day project at school, but it serves the same purpose.

## Violence: realistic vs. graphic

Juvenile mystery writers often wonder if they should include scenes that depict violence: After all, we live in a harsh world, and even young children are constantly exposed to scenes of violence on television and sometimes on the streets in their own neighborhood. Isn't it only realistic to show this in their books?

I believe that an author for children can be realistic without being overly graphic. For instance, if the young detective in a mystery story was attacked by a gang of bullies, I wouldn't encourage an author to have them burn his arms with a cigarette to get him to talk (although that might conceivably happen in real life, or in an adult mystery). However, I would accept a scene in which the gang threatened to do so; that would convey the reality and danger of the situation without portraying actual violence.

Some authors consider the mystery genre inferior and not deserving of their best efforts. I strongly disagree. It seems to me that in juvenile mysteries the characterization should be just as full-bodied, the plots just as convincing, and the writing style just as smooth as in other types of juvenile fiction. Why shortchange youngsters who enjoy a good mystery by giving them books that are lacking in literary value? That's no way to encourage a love of reading.

## Historical fiction

Since the 1950s, historical fiction for children has experienced a series of drastic ups-and-downs. Virtually every publisher of books for children issued large numbers of historical novels in the 1950s, on subjects ranging from life in Ancient Egypt, to the experiences of cabin boys who sailed with the early navigators, to the trials and tribulations of nineteenth-century American families traveling westward in wagon trains.

In the late 1960s and 1970s, however, interest in history faded. There was a slow revival in the 1980s, fueled in part by the realization that what was happening in the present could not be fully understood unless a person, young or old, had some grasp on what had happened in the past. At the same time, there arose a demand for novels that dealt with earlier periods more honestly and realistically than was true previously. No longer, for example, would librarians, reviewers, parents, or children accept stories in which all the pioneers were shining heroes and all the Native Americans villains.

Further, there is now an increased emphasis on accuracy in historical fiction. Librarians and teachers are constantly on the alert for anachronisms and factual errors in the novels they evaluate, and often they will refuse to purchase a book that fails to meet their standards, even though it may have lively, three-dimensional characters and an involving plot. To avoid rejection, historical novelists must do as much research in the periods of their stories as nonfiction writers would.

Such research shouldn't be limited to the main political events of the time—wars, revolutions, etc.—but should include the most minute details of domestic life. For instance, if toothbrushes weren't known in the twelfth century, you'd better not have your heroine using one in a story set during the reign of Eleanor of Aquitaine.

The dialogue shouldn't contain anachronisms, either. While you don't want to overload it with such antique language as "Gadzooks" and "By your leave, Madam," you shouldn't have your nineteenth-century hero saying "I've got to get my act together" or other contemporary slang expressions. You can insert a few old fashioned words to give the dialogue a period flavor, but you should rely for the most part on the same basic, simple words you'd use in the dialogue of stories set in any era. And you should avoid dialect unless it's absolutely necessary; too often it comes across as a kind of stereotyping, and it's difficult for most readers to comprehend.

When they talk of writing historical fiction, some authors think only of stories that take place in the distant past. They forget that, for children today, something that happened 10 years ago is history. The assassination of John F. Kennedy in 1963 may seem as remote to them as the assassination of Julius Caesar, and a story set in any recent period has to be researched and written with that fact in mind.

Even though Gary W. Bargar grew up in St. Louis in the 1950s, the period of his novel *Life. Is. Not. Fair.*, he read microfilms of old newspapers and magazines to refresh his memory of what was going on at the time, what TV shows were popular, and how much a tweed sports jacket cost. You'll need to do similar research if you're writing what I sometimes call a "contemporary historical novel."

But don't let yourself get too immersed in the research. While the background details of the story must be authentic, they should never overwhelm the characters and the plot, since it is these elements that will reach across time to engage the minds and emotions of present-day readers. In this regard, I recall the first reader's report at Lothrop, Lee, and Shepard on Patricia Clapp's unsolicited historical novel, *Constance: A Story of Early Plymouth*. It read: "Although all the historical details are completely convincing, it is the portrayal of the title character that makes this novel special. Constance is totally real, totally alive, and I'm sure young readers will take her to their hearts." Clearly they did, for *Constance* proved to be immensely popular, first in hardcover and later in paperback.

Remembering that reader's report, and the success of *Constance*, I always ask myself a single basic question after finishing each historical fiction manuscript that's submitted to me for consideration: "Are the central character and his or her problems so immediate that I forget I'm reading about a distant time and place?" If the answer is yes, then the story has succeeded both as history *and* as fiction.

You might do well to ask the same question of your own historical stories, either at the idea stage or after you've completed a first draft.

## Multicultural stories

The word "multicultural" first came to the fore in the early 1990s when educators stressed the need for children's books that reflected the increasing diversity of the U S. population. They called not only for more books about African-American and Hispanic life, but also for books that acknowledged the many recent immigrants from Asia, the Near East, Latin America, Eastern Europe, and the former Soviet Union.

Writers and publishers have responded to this call with a wide variety of novels that offer a more complete and authentic picture of the contemporary American scene. They have also made a serious attempt to correct the false impression of our first immigrants—the Native Americans— that many earlier children's novels conveyed. Now it's not likely that any writer would conceive of, or any editor pur- chase, a novel about the pioneer West in which all the Native American characters were portrayed as evil.

The majority of multicultural novels center on African- American and Hispanic characters, but a growing number explore the Asian-American and Muslim experience. Among the outstanding authors to emerge as part of the multicultur- al trend are Jacqueline Woodson, who sensitively depicts the feelings of adolescent African-American girls; Gary Soto, whose stories capture the imagination and vitality of young

Hispanics; and Sook Nyul Choi, whose memories of the Korean War add a special poignancy to her novels about a girl caught up in that struggle.

A debate continues as to whether writers who are not members of a particular race or ethnic group have the insights and knowledge needed to portray it convincingly. Many critics assert that they do not. Others say those critics fail to give enough credit to the role imagination plays in the writing of fiction. Meanwhile, Caucasian writers such as Bruce Brooks, Mary Stolz, and Paula Fox have written successful novels featuring African-American characters. And African-American writers like Virginia Hamilton have included white characters in their books.

There are many factors to consider when approaching multicultural story material. If you're not an insider, it might be extremely difficult to bring off a story about, say, a teenage Chinese American boy told from his point of view. But if you're planning a contemporary school story set in a small northern city, and aim to present a realistic picture of life in that community, you'll no doubt want to have more than a few African-American characters in the cast. Depending on the city and the immigrant groups it has attracted, you may also want to include some Hispanic, Asian-American, or Muslim characters.

Remember, too, that the word "multicultural" is not limited to people of color. Taken in a broader sense, it embraces all the many nationalities that have helped to shape the United States. So if your ancestors came from Scandinavia, and you weave some of their Christmas customs into a novel, it will be as much an example of multiculturalism as a story centered on Haitian or Vietnamese customs.

## Fantasies and science fiction

If beginning writers who didn't know the range and scope of the children's book field were asked to describe a typical juvenile novel, many would be likely to think of such classics as *Alice in Wonderland* and *Winnie the Pooh* and say "fantasy." That probably explains why so many novice authors attempt to write a fantasy as their first venture into juvenile fiction.

In my experience, a fantasy is the hardest type of juvenile novel to write, and also the hardest to bring off successfully. But what about all the wonderful fantasies for children that have been published, you may ask. Just look at E. B. White's masterpieces, *Stuart Little* and *Charlotte's Web*, or Richard Adams's magnificent animal fantasy, *Watership Down*, or Mary Norton's delightful tale of miniature people, *The Borrowers*; not to mention that contemporary publishing phenomenon, the Harry Potter books, and the immensely popular stories by Lemony Snicket.

Yes, look at them; then examine what makes them successful and ask yourself that most painful but necessary of questions: Do I have the talent required to write a story that will be the equal of these books? For, in the field of fantasy and its first cousin, science fiction, nothing less than the best will do.

## Originality is essential

Let's take a look at some of the special requirements of fantasy and science fiction writing—and why they're so daunting.

1. *A high degree of imagination*, both in the conception and execution of the story. In no other fictional genre is originality so essential.

2. *The ability to create a fantasy world that's as believable and convincing as the real world.* This isn't as easy as it may sound. For example, if you're writing a novel like *The Borrowers*, about miniature creatures, you have to make sure that everything in their world is in the proper scale. You can't have a six-inch-high man run down the path and mail a letter in a conventional mailbox. He could never reach it, let

alone pull down the slot cover. Nor, at the other extreme, can you have a 12-foot-tall giant enter an ordinary theater and sit comfortably in a people-sized seat to watch the movie. You'll have to think carefully about every single detail in your imaginary world to make sure it's plausible on its own terms.

3. *A subtly handled theme and fully rounded characters.* Many authors of fantasies have an axe to grind or a moral point they're eager to make. A frequent theme is the contrast between our corrupt world and a more perfect one, located either in the distant past or the far future. Or the characters may find themselves caught up in a cosmic clash between the forces of good and the forces of evil; *The Wizard of Oz* and the Harry Potter books are good examples of the latter situation.

The danger in trying to write such stories is that the authors may allow the moral to become too obvious and fail to pay sufficient attention to the characterizations. As a result, their heroes often seem like cardboard cutouts and the villains are equally one-dimensional. These authors forget that the theme of a fantasy, to be effective, should be subtly introduced and the characters developed with as much depth as those in any other type of novel.

4. *A compact manuscript.* I don't know why, but the manuscripts of many fantasy novels I see are at least twice as long as their realistic counterparts. That wouldn't be a problem if the authors were as inventive as J. K. Rowling, creator of the Harry Potter stories, but too many writers run out of steam somewhere along the way, yet keep on going. The result: novels that are much too rambling and verbose to hold the attention of young readers.

5. *A fine literary style.* "Style" is a word that's bandied about a great deal, but what exactly do we mean by it? Webster's defines literary style as "The manner or mode of expression in language; the way of putting thoughts into

words." It goes on to add a further definition: "Distinction, excellence, originality, and character in any form of artistic or literary expression: as, this author lacks *style*."

Style is an important element in all types of writing, but it's especially important in fantasy. If you're describing the Emerald City of Oz or its equivalent, your language has to rise to the occasion. It can't seem forced, however. Nothing is more depressing than to come across an overly "poetic" description in a fantasy manuscript and sense that the author is trying terribly hard to be "stylish." It can be as painful as seeing a man or woman wearing unsuitable clothes just because they happen to be in vogue at the moment.

So, if you're writing a fantasy, be aware of the need for imaginative writing, but remember that in writing as in other activities it's always better to be yourself. Your own style—plain or ornate, direct or convoluted—will inevitably emerge and be more effective than a strained attempt at "fine writing."

## Science fiction requirements

The requirements for science fiction are much the same as those for fantasies, with a few additions. Since science fiction stories often center on visions of future worlds, either in space or on earth, the authors need to have a firm grip on the principles of science and technology. However, the technological details must never be permitted to overwhelm the story: lengthy technical descriptions are as off-putting to readers as lengthy exposition of any kind.

After studying the above requirements, be as honest as you can about your writing abilities before you embark on a fantasy or science fiction novel. If you have what you believe is a marvelous idea for such a novel, and are convinced you possess the skills to carry it off, by all means move forward with the project. But if you find it difficult to visualize magical kingdoms or an advanced civilization in another galaxy, or if you lack the verbal facility to bring them to life, you're likely to spend months or even years writing a manuscript that no one will want to publish. Better to survey the field—and yourself—carefully beforehand, and invest that time and energy in a different kind of novel.

## Graphic novels

One of the newest fiction categories has some of the oldest roots. Graphic novels can trace their origins back to the great cathedrals of the Middle Ages, in which the main events in the life of Christ were portrayed on window panels of brilliantly colored glass.

Over the centuries, telling a story in visual panels left the church and entered the secular realm via such works as "The Rake's Progress" by the great English artist William Hogarth. This form of storytelling reached a peak in the popular comic strips of the twentieth century, many of which were anything but comic. As a boy, I delighted in the adventures of "Dick Tracy" and "Terry and the Pirates," enjoying the details in the drawings as much as the narratives they pictured.

Comic strips like these and "Peanuts" exerted a strong influence on the artists, including Art Spiegelman, Chris Ware, and Robert Clowes, who pioneered the graphic novel form. Some critics dismissed their early efforts as little more than "literary comic books," but others perceived the books' unique qualities. Spiegelman's *Maus*, a Holocaust story in which Nazi cats terrorize Jewish mice, won a Pulitzer Prize. Clowes's *Ghost World*, about two high school girls whose friendship is threatened by outside forces, was made into a popular movie.

While most pioneers of the graphic novel were men, several women have made important contributions also. One of the latter is author-illustrator Marjane Satrapi, whose poignant story of a young girl growing up in Iran, *Persepolis*, has won her many fans.

These graphic novels and others like them were published originally for an adult audience. It wasn't long, though, before they were discovered by young adult readers who responded strongly to the combination of involving narratives and striking visuals. Children's and young adult publishers recognized the books' appeal and soon established separate divisions to develop graphic novels designed especially for middle-graders and young adults.

Many children's writers would like to try their hand at stories for graphic novels. So far, though, the best examples have come from author-illustrators who are able to create a unified product in which the text and illustrations work hand-in-hand from the start. Reflecting this fact, those in charge of the graphic novel programs at several publishers are art directors, not editors.

That's not to say that writers who are not illustrators will forever be excluded from the graphic novel field. Perhaps it will develop along lines similar to those that characterize the production of many comic books, where a writer thinks up the story, an illustrator draws each scene in ink, and another artist colors in the panels.

In any event, whoever writes the text will need to visualize it down to the last detail. The end result will probably be much more like the script for a TV show or a movie than a conventional book manuscript. Exchanges of dialogue will have to be interspersed with detailed descriptions of what each panel in the story will depict, and whether the scene will be a long shot, a medium shot, or a closeup. The author may even go so far as to spell out the angle from which each panel should be drawn.

The illustrator or the editor/art director may well differ with the author over what should be shown in some of the panels, and how best to show it. But in the meantime, the author will have fulfilled his or her main task—to provide the others on the creative team with a clear blueprint for the finished book.

So far, many of the most successful graphic novels, like Marjane Satrapi's *Persepolis*, have been highly personal, if not autobiographical, with the central characters indulging in frequent asides to the reader. But the movie-like nature of the graphic novel lends itself to a much wider range of subject matter, from historical epics to slapstick comedy. The emphasis on dramatic visuals makes the genre seem especially well-suited to horror and suspense stories.

At this point, halfway through the first decade of the 21st century, the graphic novel is very much a work-in-progress. It'll be fascinating to see how the concept evolves, and the role that children's and young adult writers will play in its development.

## New visions, unique voices

Whatever fiction genre you pursue, whether a light contemporary novel, a work of historical fiction, or a venture into fantasy, you'll be well advised to follow your own path. The way to stand out if you're a newcomer is not to imitate someone else's past success but to present a vision and voice that are uniquely your own.

An excellent example of a writer who has accomplished this is Karen Cushman. She was completely unknown until 1994, when her first book, *Catherine, Called Birdy*, was published to widespread acclaim and was named a Newbery Honor Book. The following year, her second book, *The Midwife's Apprentice*, walked off with the Newbery Medal itself. Not since the debut of E. L. Konigsburg almost 30 years earlier had a new writer of children's fiction made such a smashing debut.

It's noteworthy that Cushman achieved her triumph with two novels that violate some widely accepted notions of what's marketable. Both of her books are works of historical fiction, a category that many writers, editors, and marketing directors were dismissing as virtually unsaleable a few short years ago. Not only that, but the novels are set in medieval England, a period and locale little-known to most of today's teenage readers. And these books use a flavorsome but often unfamiliar vocabulary.

Outweighing any possible drawbacks, though, are Cushman's obvious fascination with her subject matter, her skills as a storyteller, and her ability to reach across the centuries and grip the imaginations of her readers. These strengths enabled her books to scale the heights of the children's book field. They also led to impressive sales in both the library and bookstore markets.

There's a lesson to be learned here by all fiction writers, both new and established. If you ignore the conventional wisdom and write a story based on material you know and care about, chances are your work will attract an editor's attention, even in a crowded and difficult marketplace.

 Chapter Nine

# The Wide World of Picture Books

By far the largest number of submissions that children's book publishers receive are stories intended for picture book treatment. At the publishing house where I work, for example, I'd estimate that of the seven thousand or so submissions that we get in an average year, at least 3,500 are texts for picture books.

These manuscripts may be one page long or fifteen, but all the authors think they can be turned into picture books. Often, the manuscripts are accompanied by a cover letter saying the author's children, or grandchildren, loved the story when it was read aloud to them. That may be true—the children probably loved the feel of Grandma's lap and the sound of her voice—but unfortunately 99% of these stories could never be published as picture books. Why? Because their authors don't understand the form and its rigid requirements.

To begin with, there are many different kinds of picture books, geared to several different age groups. Here, we'll discuss the most popular types, starting with board books for the youngest audience.

## Board books

The first books toddlers six months to two years old usually see are board books—so-called because they are produced on sturdy cardboard pages that little hands can't easily tear apart.

Board books are generally only 12 to 24 pages long and introduce young children to the simplest of concepts: colors, sizes, shapes, basic items of clothing, etc. If they have a story line, it is minimal. The texts often consist of only one or two words per page, and the entire manuscript may not be more than 50 words.

Since the illustrations are so important in board books, many of the most popular series have been created by illustrators who are also authors, such as Dick Bruna, Rosemary Wells, and Helen Oxenbury. Other board books are put together by publishing entrepreneurs called packagers, who conceive of a series of six or eight titles, line up established writers and illustrators to produce them, and sell the entire package to a publisher.

Because of these practices, the board book area is one of the hardest for a new writer to break into. Before planning or writing a board book of your own, you should study published ones carefully to make sure your idea has something new and different to contribute to this crowded field. Then you should query publishers of board books to see if they'd be interested in considering your material.

## Novelty books

A novelty, or toy, book is basically one that relies for its overall impact on a special effect or movable part. These include flaps that lift, a glittery or fabric-covered surface, or something that pops up from the page and creates a 3-D illustration.

Pop-up books have a long history, dating back to the early years of the twentieth century, and Dorothy Kunhardt's enduring classic *Pat the Bunny* spawned a host of fabric-covered imitations in the 1940s. Novelty books dwindled in importance during the decades when the library market dominated the children's book field, but they've made a strong comeback in recent years as the technology for producing them has advanced and publishers have placed increased emphasis on the retail market.

As with any picture book, a novelty book starts with a fresh and engaging story idea that can best be realized with the aid of the novelty element. It helps in conceiving a novelty book to have a clear idea of how the special effects can be achieved, and to make a cardboard dummy or prototype of the book that can be submitted to the publisher along with a copy of the text. Most novelty books are geared to preschoolers, so the text will need to be brief but flavorful.

A majority of novelty books are developed by packagers who sell their finished product to trade publishers. Before attempting to market your novelty book, you'll need to research the Internet and the annual reference book, "Literary Marketplace," to find out which packagers are active in the novelty field. Once you have a list in hand, you can query the packagers to see if they'd be interested in considering your project.

The novelty book field is a hard one to crack. But if you have a truly original idea—and one whose special effects can be replicated effectively and economically—you'll stand a good chance of finding a publishing home for it.

## Celebrity picture books

This is a category for which most of you won't qualify, but you should be aware of it because picture books written by celebrities in other fields have become, for better or worse, a significant part of the children's book scene.

The reason for this development is simple. As publishers have sought ways to increase bookstore sales, they've discovered that casual buyers often respond more quickly to a picture book authored by a familiar name, whether it be an actor like John Lithgow, a TV personality like Maria Shriver, a politician like Ed Koch, the former mayor of New York, or a singer like Madonna. In some instances, the celebrity does not actually write the book. Instead, they are solicited for an idea that is turned over to someone on the publisher's staff, often the editor, to put down on paper.

If you're not a celebrity, there's no way you can compete in this arena. But you should be aware of the phenomenon, since it can affect your chances of selling your own manuscript. For every slot on a publisher's list that's occupied by a celebrity picture book means one less slot available for a book by a new or little-known author. And so, if you want to overcome this particular type of unfair competition, you'll need to be even more demanding of yourself, and submit only the best and most original work of which you're capable.

## Picture books for children two to five

These books are usually longer than board books, averaging 32 pages. They are sometimes described as "pure" picture books because the illustrations occupy a far greater proportion of the books than the text. But a good text is essential to the success of the books since all picture books—no matter how heavily illustrated—depend on their texts for structure and point.

Beginning authors often make the mistake of thinking pure picture books are easy to write because the manuscripts are so short—generally no more than two or three double-spaced typewritten pages. Actually, they're as hard to do well as a poem, since each word counts and must be precisely the right one for the idea or emotion you are trying to convey.

Beginners also tend to choose clichéd plot lines for their picture book stories. Some those editors see most frequently are: the little animal (or child) who defies his mother, runs away, gets scared by something, and learns that home is best after all; or the protagonist—animal or human—who wishes he were something else, tries several alternatives, and ends up deciding he'd rather be himself; or the child who has a marvelous nighttime adventure, only to wake and discover it was just a dream. Some writers are able to breathe new life into such overused story situations, but most authors would do well to avoid them.

The pure picture book category embraces a wide range of subject matter. Here are some of the most common types:

1. *Concept Books.* When people think of concept books for young children, alphabet and counting books usually come to mind first because they're the most prevalent. But other types of concept books are popular, too—for example, Tana Hoban's series of photographic concept books in which she encourages young readers to take a close-up look at familiar objects.

Concept books bridge the fiction and nonfiction genres, and in fact are often classified as nonfiction. Because there are so many concept books on the market—especially alphabet and counting books—they need an original idea and slant if they are to compete successfully. Mary Elting and Michael Folsom succeeded in finding such an approach in their alphabet guessing game, *Q Is for Duck.* ("Q is for duck. Why? Because a duck quacks. ") Author-illustrator Catherine Stock also succeeded in her book *Alexander's Midnight Snack: A Little Elephant's ABC.* Waking up hungry at midnight, Alexander tiptoes downstairs to the kitchen where he finds the makings of a giant snack that introduce all the letters of the alphabet. What did Ms. Stock come up with for X? An X-ray showing what Alexander's stomach looked like after he'd eaten all the alphabetical foods.

If you're thinking of writing an alphabet book, you'd be well advised to put it to the X-test to see how you're going to get over that particular hurdle, which has defeated many otherwise promising alphabet book ideas. You should also ask yourself if your idea is really suited to alphabet-age youngsters of, say, three to five. Far too many authors of alphabet books use material beyond the grasp or interest of young children—*A Is for Architect*, for example. Nor do such books appeal to older children, most of whom would find them "babyish."

Story frameworks like the one in *Alexander's Midnight Snack* add another dimension to concept books, but they must grow naturally out of the material and not seem to be imposed on it. Whether fictional elements are introduced or not, the best concept books are carefully shaped by their authors and have strong beginnings, a mid-section that sustains interest, and usually a twist at the end to round off the book in a satisfying fashion. With structure like this, your concept book—whether it be an alphabet book, a counting book, or an introduction to colors—stands a much better chance of catching an editor's eye, and later on, the attention of children in libraries and bookstores.

2. *Animal fantasies.* Children love to read about animals and look at pictures of them. Many children also find it easier to accept the portrayal of strong emotions—anger, jealousy, etc.—if they're expressed by animals instead of children, as in Russell Hoban's much loved stories about Frances, a little badger. The children's distance from the animals makes identification with their emotions less threatening.

Animal fantasies demand many of the same things from writers as fantasy novels. The basic idea of the story should be imaginative; the fantasy world depicted and the behavior of the animal characters within it must be believable on their own terms; the moral of the story, while clear, should never be hammered home in an obvious fashion; and the writing style should be flowing and graceful, brightened by touches of humor and lyricism.

Although the animal fantasy genre has the advantages of imagination and child appeal, it can present many pitfalls to the unwary writer. Here are several things to guard against if you're thinking of writing an animal fantasy: (a) Don't rely on cute names like Billy Beaver and Wanda Weasel for characterization. It's what the animals *do* in the story that will make them memorable, not what they're called. (b) Avoid cuteness in the dialogue, too. As for having animals talk in picture books, it all depends on what they have to say. The *content* of the dialogue is what's important, not the mere fact that it's an animal who is speaking.

3. *"Here-and-Now" stories.* Some librarians and teachers still call realistic picture book texts "Here-and-Now Stories." This expression dates back to the 1930s when Lucy Sprague Mitchell of the Bank Street College of Education wrote that, along with the classic and modern fantasy tales, small children needed to have stories that reflected the here and now of their everyday world.

Author-illustrator Lois Lenski proved herself to be an early master of the realistic genre with a series of books that included *Cowboy Small*. Charlotte Zolotow has continued the tradition in such brief but probing texts as *William's Doll*, about a boy who craves a doll even though some of his friends and family think it's "sissy," and *A Tiger Called Thomas*, about another boy who overcomes his shyness when he dons a tiger costume to go trick-or-treating on Halloween.

Realistic picture books can also be a vehicle for the depiction of multicultural subjects. Black author-artist Donald Crews demonstrated this in his book *Bigmama's*, a loving evocation of summer days he spent as a boy at his grandmother's home in the South.

One of the most skilled and prolific writers of the realistic picture book today is Eve Bunting. Her stories run the gamut from the lightly humorous (*A Perfect Father's Day*, about a little girl who treats Dad to all of *her* favorite things) to intimate family dramas (*The Wednesday Surprise*, in which a granddaughter helps her immigrant grandmother learn to read) to works that explore sensitive contemporary issues like homelessness (*Fly Away Home*, which tells of a boy and his father reduced to living in a big city airport).

Editors are always on the lookout for realistic stories like these that project the child's world at home, in the neighborhood, or at school in a fresh, imaginative way. However, they receive far too many manuscripts of the "I Go to the Supermarket" variety that aren't real stories, but merely a dull description of a place or an event. Here-and-Now stories should have the same basic elements as other kinds of picture book stories: an intriguing opening, a well-developed middle, and, if possible, a clever final twist at the end.

Because the picture book form is so compressed, a writer can't afford to ramble around, as a novelist may, until he or she arrives at just the right ending. Knowing this, many writers of Here-and-Now stories and other types of picture books start with the climax of the story and work backward. In fact, Eve Bunting says she often writes the last paragraph of a picture book text before she writes the first.

While the subject matter in a Here-and-Now story may be mundane, the writing should never be. Without straining for effect, the story should be written in rhythmical prose and feature vivid images and turns of phrase. As in all picture books, each word is important in a Here-and-Now story. And because there are so few words on a page, they tend to jump out at the reader. Consequently, any that seem awkward or inappropriate will be much more noticeable than they would on the denser-type page of a junior novel.

Besides being well written, a Here-and-Now story should contain several different settings and other good illustration possibilities if it's to be considered seriously by a picture book editor. For example, a manuscript may have a charming tone and include many appealing, lifelike touches. But if the entire action takes place in a kitchen where a mother and daughter are baking cookies, the editor will probably decide that the story has too little illustration potential to warrant picture book treatment, especially at today's book prices. The editor might suggest that the author try the story with a children's magazine, where it could be published effectively with just one or two illustrations.

Surprisingly, considering the widespread appeal of realistic picture book stories, editors receive far fewer submissions of this kind than they do in the animal fantasy and concept book categories. This seems a pity for, in my experience, most beginning picture book authors would stand a much better chance of selling a skillfully told Here-and-Now story.

4. *Mood pieces.* These are texts that attempt to capture the essence of an experience, a mood, in poetic language if not actual poetry. Mood pieces first came to the fore in the 1940s with the publication of such books as Alvin Tresselt's 1947 Caldecott Medal winner, *White Snow, Bright Snow* (illustrated by Roger Duvoisin), which depicts a winter snowfall and how it affects a large cast of characters.

Like *White Snow, Bright Snow*, many successful mood pieces have centered on nature themes. Tresselt himself wrote a number of them in the 1950s and 1960s, culminating in *Hide-and-Seek Fog*, which also was illustrated by Roger Duvoisin and was a Caldecott Honor Book in 1965. The latter title followed a typical mood piece pattern, opening with a scene of children playing on a Cape Cod beach on a sunny day. Then a fog rolls in, blanketing the beach and the summer houses, and the children must be content with indoor activities. At last the fog lifts, and the text comes full circle with the children back on the sunny beach on the book's last page.

Mood pieces fell somewhat out of favor in the 1970s and early 1980s, perhaps because many subjects had been treated in more than one book, and some in six or seven. After all, how many evocations of a rainy day does a library or bookstore need on its shelves? But an outstanding mood piece can still make an impact. This was demonstrated by Jane Yolen's Caldecott Medal Winner, *Owl Moon*, illustrated by John Schoenherr, which lovingly portrays a girl and her father going out in search of owls on a cold winter night.

At first glance, a mood piece may seem easy to write because there is no story line, and no need for character development. Actually, they're more difficult to bring off than other types of picture book stories, because, in the absence of a plot, the young reader's attention has to be captured and held solely by the excitement of the experience recounted and the quality of the writing. Mood pieces also require even more distinguished illustrations than some other kinds of picture books—drawings or paintings that can project the natural beauties described in the text.

Ordinariness of subject matter is the most common flaw in mood piece manuscripts. If you're thinking of writing one, begin by studying a selection of outstanding mood books in a library or bookstore to make sure you have a truly original idea. Yet another version of *A Day at the Beach*, or something similar, probably won't be considered a strong enough candidate for publication in today's highly competitive picture book market, no matter how well it's written.

5. *Retold nursery and folk tales, and picture book versions of songs.* When you walk into the children's section of a bookstore, your eye is likely to be caught first by a display of new picture book versions of such classic nursery and folk-tales as *The Little Red Hen* and *The Three Bears*. The display may also include illustrated renditions of favorite children's songs like "Roll Over" and "Papa's Going to Buy Me a Mockingbird."

Seeing books like these, many authors decide there must be a large market for retellings and hurry home to their computers to dash one off. Later, they're disappointed when their manuscripts come back from publisher after publisher, and they can't understand why. The answer is that almost all retellings of nursery and folktales start with the illustrator or the publisher, not with the author. The illustrator is seeking a vehicle to display his talents, and since most such tales are in the public domain, he also sees illustrating one as a way to get the full royalty on the book instead of having to share the income with an author. If the text of the original tale needs cutting or rewriting, this is generally done by the illustrator in tandem with the editor, or sometimes by an established freelancer who is engaged for a flat fee.

In light of these realities, I usually advise authors to concentrate on original material instead of retelling a familiar tale—unless, of course, they've unearthed a wonderful old story that, for some reason, has been overlooked for generations. Even then, it's wise to go on the Internet or check the title section of the latest edition of *Children's Books in Print*, available in most public libraries, to make sure other picture book versions of the tale don't exist.

Although you may never retell an old tale, they are still worth careful study in terms of structure as you develop your own original stories. For example, the cumulative effects that delight children in tales like *Henny Penny* and *The Gingerbread Boy* can be put to good advantage in a contemporary story. So can the pattern of threes that works so well in stories ranging from *The Three Little Pigs* and *The Three Billy Goats Gruff* to *The Three Wishes*. You may be writing about a girl who has to perform three tasks at home or school before she wins a reward instead of a prince who has to overcome three obstacles, including a fire-breathing dragon, before he wins the hand of the princess. But the classic pattern of your story is likely to be just as satisfying to young participants in a story hour today as it was to listeners gathered around a Celtic campfire 1,500 years ago.

## Picture story books for ages five to eight

From concept books, to retold tales, to realistic stories, picture story books cover the same broad spectrum of subjects as do pure picture books. There are only four basic differences between the two categories.

1. Picture story books are aimed at a somewhat older audience than the pure picture book—five-to-eight-year-olds instead of two-to-five-year-olds.

2. Because they're written for older children with longer attention spans, the stories may have more complex characterization and plots than those for the younger picture book set. Examples of outstanding picture story books include Vera B. Williams' *A Chair for My Mother*, Emily Arnold McCully's *Mirette on the High Wire*, William Joyce's *Dinosaur Bob*, and Joanna Cole's popular stories about the Magic School Bus.

3. Reflecting their greater complexity, texts of picture story books are longer, running from four to eight double-spaced manuscript pages and sometimes more. As books, they may extend in length to 48 pages instead of the usual 32, and the text often takes up as much space in the book as the illustrations.

4. Whereas most of the retold tales that appear as pure picture books are animal fantasies like *The Three Little Pigs*, retellings of fairy tales such as *Rumpelstiltskin* and *Snow White* predominate in the picture story book area. As with the retellings of nursery tales, most of the new versions of fairy tales are done either by the illustrator or the editor.

There's also a limited market in the picture story book category for original tales cast in the traditional folk and fairy tale mold. Jane Yolen, for one, has made a name for herself with stories of this type including *Greyling, The Girl Who Loved the Wind*, and the Caldecott Honor Book, *The Emperor and the Kite*, illustrated by Ed Young. But it's a tough market for the new author to break into, since an original tale, like a fantasy novel, demands a high degree of imagination and writing skill. Most beginners would probably do better to master the craft of the realistic story before trying their hands at original tales.

# Picture books for older children

Earlier, in the section on picture book biographies, I mentioned that the audience for picture books has expanded greatly in recent years. No longer does it end with children of seven or eight. Now, for some books, it extends upward to the eight-to-twelve-year-old group, and even to young adults. While this trend is most apparent in the nonfiction area, it can apply to some fiction titles also.

*Fiction picture books*
Picture story books with appeal to older as well as younger children include David Macaulay's Caldecott Medal-winning *Black and White*, which tells four different stories simultaneously; D. B. Johnson's *Henry Hikes to Fitchburg*, an affectionate tale of a bear named Henry, whose actions echo those of Henry David Thoreau; and Chris Van Allsburg's *The Mysteries of Harris Burdick*. The latter's vaguely menacing illustrations encourage youngsters of all ages to expand on the brief text passages and invent their own stories.

The three books mentioned above were all created by author-illustrators, but they can provide stimulation and impetus to writers as well. What qualities made these books work with older children and young adults? First, and most important, none of them is in any way "cute." Their concerns aren't limited to those of young children, or small animals, either. For example, Henry in *Henry Hikes to Fitchburg* isn't just a bear; he's actually an ursine standin for Thoreau himself, something older readers should find amusing.

The books also embody imaginative concepts that can be appreciated by a broad age range. The haunting vignettes in *The Mysteries of Harris Burdick* would no doubt trigger different stories from eight-year-olds than they would from thirteen-year-olds. But both age groups would probably enjoy the book just as much.

*Nonfiction Picture Books*

A multitude of topics in many different subject areas are currently being explored by the authors of nonfiction picture books. Stuart Murphy introduces the basic concepts of mathematics in a series of instructive and entertaining titles. Sy Montgomery describes the work of scientists in the field in such books as *The Tarantula Scientist* and *The Snake Scientist.* And Lynn Curlee, in books like *Parthenon* and *Rushmore*, brings history to life by focusing on some of the world's architectural wonders.

Focus is the key to the success of all these books, and it was something I kept constantly in mind when I was writing my nonfiction picture book, *Secrets of the Sphinx.* While maintaining a close focus on the monumental creature, I was able to weave in related material on the history of Egypt, the lives and working conditions of the laborers who shaped the great statue, and the conservation methods that scientists today are employing to preserve the Sphinx. At the same time, the tight focus helped me to limit the length of the text to 20 manuscript pages, which I knew would work within the strict confines of a 48-page picture book.

Beyond finding the right focus, there are other considerations you'll need to bear in mind in planning and writing a nonfiction picture book

1. There may be no new subjects under the sun, but there are many new approaches you can take to almost any subject. For example, countless nonfiction books about the pyramids of ancient Egypt have been written for young readers, but when I checked the Internet and the *Subject Guide to Children's Books in Print* I could find none devoted exclusively to the Sphinx. That encouraged me to pursue the idea, write a proposal for it, and market the proposal successfully.

2. As with all picture books, you should remember the needs of the illustrator and build a variety of different scenes and locations into the text. In the Sphinx book, after opening

with a description of the monument today, I flashed back to ancient Egypt long before the Sphinx was conceived, and traced in a few paragraphs the social and architectural developments that led to its construction. This provided the artist with many different illustration possibilities.

3. Because I wanted every word in the brief text to count, I tried to make sure that each paragraph added several new facts to the story of the Sphinx. At the same time, I seized every opportunity to enliven the writing with touches of humor, drama, and even lyricism. In that way, I hoped to avoid the danger that threatens all writers of nonfiction: that they'll end up with a text that is completely accurate but deadly dull.

4. As emphasized before, appropriate back matter is a vital element in nonfiction for every age level. But it's especially important in nonfiction picture books where there's usually no room in the main text for digressions that can add texture and richness to the topic. With this in mind, I resisted the temptation to include the Greek myth of Oedipus and the Sphinx in the body of the book, but found room for it in the back matter, where it serves as a vivid example of a different kind of Sphinx.

Whatever type of picture book you're writing, fiction or nonfiction, you'll need to think visually from the time you get the idea until you complete the final draft of the manuscript. The next chapter lays out some methods you can employ to accomplish this essential goal.

 Chapter Ten

# Visualizing the Picture Book Text

Whether you're planning a pure picture book for younger children or a picture story book for an older audience, your manuscript will have to meet certain basic requirements that are common to all picture books. Here are some hints on how to shape your material so that it will fulfill these requirements.

## Think visually

Even if you're not an artist, you should think visually about your story from the start. You may find it useful—many authors have—to type out the texts of several favorite picture books page by page. This should help you to see (a) how economical the writing is; (b) how the stories are paced; and (c) how much the authors left to their illustrators.

You'll probably discover that, especially in stories for younger children, there are few if any passages of straight description. While the author concentrates on the essentials of action and dialogue, it is the illustrator's responsibility to convey the color of a desert sky at night, the other passengers on a crowded bus, or the various flowers in a springtime garden.

## Make a dummy of your story

After you've completed the first draft of your story, photocopy the manuscript, mark it as to which passages you think should appear on each page, and then make up a rough dummy of the book. You may never show this dummy to anyone else, but you can learn a lot from it that will help you when you're revising and polishing your manuscript.

Most picture books, as we've said before, are 32 pages long, but the text and illustrations usually occupy no more than 28 of these. The remaining four are taken up with what is known as "front matter." Here, for you to use as a guide when you're making your dummy, is how the sequence generally runs:

> *Page 1*—The half title. The only type on this page is the book's title; sometimes a small spot illustration accompanies it.
>
> *Pages 2 and 3*—These pages are usually devoted to what is called a "double-spread title page." This simply means that the title type often crosses both pages, with an illustration on page 2, and the author's, illustrator's, and publisher's names on page 3, the right-hand page.
>
> *Page 4*—The copyright page. The book's copyright notice appears on this page, along with other bibliographical data. If you and the illustrator want to have dedications in the book, they will probably appear on this page also, above the copyright notice.
>
> *Pages 5-32*—The text and illustrations.

Although the above is the standard page sequence for most picture books, there can be some variations. For instance, room must be left at the end of many nonfiction picture books for the sort of additional material described in Chapters 3 and 9, and this often extends the length of the book to 40 or even 48 pages.

Space may have to be reserved for extra items in fictional picture books also. If the book is a retelling of a little-known folktale from a particular culture, librarians and teachers will expect you to include a note identifying the source. There may be room for this on the copyright page; if not, you and your editor will have to find a spot for it elsewhere.

Or perhaps the story is based on an incident that actually happened to your grandfather or grandmother when they were children. If so, you'll probably want to let readers know this in an Author's Note appearing at either the beginning or end of the book. And a page will have to be set aside for it.

Despite the problems involved with such variations, there are many ways you can make the basic picture book format work in your favor when you're planning and writing the manuscript. For example, knowing that the text begins on page 5 in most picture books, skilled picture book authors will often start their stories with a brief, intriguing paragraph of no more than two or three typewritten lines that they know will fit comfortably on this page. And they make sure that the paragraph contains the sort of action or emotion that will inspire a vivid illustration.

## Building suspense

Practiced authors also use the dummy format to help build suspense into their stories. One of the best ways to do this is to take full advantage of the turn from one page to another. For example, in *Three Ducks Went Wandering*, Ron Roy gets his story going in the first few pages when three little ducks disobey their mother and leave the barnyard to see the world. Then Roy uses the page turns to heighten the drama as the little ducks escape from one threatening situation after another, only to be confronted by an even more dangerous one.

On pages 6 and 7 the ducks have wandered into the enclosure of a big, angry bull. The text reads, "With a snort the bull lowered his head and charged at the ducks," and there's a dramatic illustration by Paul Galdone of the bull coming straight toward the defenseless creatures. Eagerly, the reader turns the page to find out what will happen next and sees a picture of the bull crashing into the fence, while the little ducks waddle safely under the lowest bar.

Child readers and listeners are relieved, of course, but Roy doesn't want them to be so relieved that they'll lose interest in the story. So he relies again on the dummy format to generate fresh suspense. On pages 12 and 13, the text reads: "The three ducks gobbled up the grasshoppers, and then went wandering on through the woods, RIGHT IN FRONT OF. . . ." Right in front of what? Once more the reader turns the page to discover what the fearsome creature may be, and interest in the story is securely maintained.

Page turns can help you tell your story in other ways. You can use them to raise the emotional level of a scene: "Maria raced to the door. . . (Turn the page) . . . and there was Daddy, home at last." They can also make a funny moment even funnier: "Shawn and Tony put a seventeenth block on top of their tower. Suddenly it started to topple. . . (Turn the page) . . . and before they could stop it, the whole tower came crashing down." There are all sorts of things you can do with page turns, once you get the knack of working them logically and naturally into your picture book story.

Making a dummy will also help you to pace the story more effectively. If you suddenly find yourself with five paragraphs of text on a page, whereas most of the other pages have had only one or two, chances are the passage would benefit from cutting and tightening. Ask yourself, "Is that paragraph of description really necessary? Does the dialogue between the two boys in the scene go on too long?" Facing the problem in the dummy will enable you to improve the manuscript before you submit it to an editor.

# The final twist

One of the most important pages in any picture book is page
32, the last page. And the most crucial turn of all is the one
from page 31 to page 32. Ideally, every picture book should
end with a final twist or surprise, and this climactic turn to
page 32 is the best place to put it.

A good example can be found in Anna Grossnickle
Hines's *It's Just Me, Emily*. All through the book, from morning until mid-afternoon, a mother and her little daughter
have been playing an imaginative hide-and-seek guessing
game. The daughter makes different animal sounds, the
mother guesses what they are, and the little girl says over
and over, "No! It's just me, Emily." Then, on pages 30 and 31,
the house becomes strangely quiet. The text on page 30
reads, "No thumping or bumping. No howls and no yowls.
No giggles or wiggles," and the mother is shown getting up
from her sewing machine and looking for Emily.

Under a picture of the mother searching on page 31, the
following text appears: "Not a sound . . . not a peep. 'Do you
think it could be . . .? Shhhhhh!'" The reader turns to page
32, and Hines delivers the book's final, gentle twist. Both the
reader and her mother see Emily napping peacefully on the
rug behind a wing chair, and beneath the picture are
Mother's words: "Yes. It's just Emily. "

Depending on the nature of the material, all sorts of
twists can make satisfying resolutions for picture book stories. The twist can be as simple as that classic line that ends
so many fairy tales: "And they lived happily ever after." Or it
can be as complicated as the solution to a picture book mystery. But whatever it is, you should have it in mind from the
time you conceive your story. And, whether you make a
dummy of your story or not, you should plan for this final
twist to appear on page 32—preferably expressed in as few
words as possible.

## Should I show my dummy to an editor?

Authors often ask if they should submit their rough dummies to editors along with their picture book manuscripts. In most cases, the answer is "No." However, there are some instances when letting the editor know how you visualize the book is absolutely essential.

1. *When the structure and pacing of the story depend on a turn-the-page guessing game format.* For example, when Beatrice Schenk de Regniers submitted the manuscript of *It Does Not Say Meow*, she needed to tell the editor that she intended the clues in verse to appear on a double-page spread, and the name of the animal to be revealed on the spread that followed.

2. *When the identity of an important character or other element is deliberately withheld from the reader, but must be known by the illustrator.* Eve Bunting had this problem with her story *Scary, Scary Halloween*. She solved it by telling the editor in an introductory note that the characters watching a parade of Halloween trick-or-treaters are a mother cat and her kittens, although readers don't discover this until the book's next-to-last page.

3. *When a significant action is not described in the text, but must be shown in the illustrations.* In Carol Carrick's *Big Old Bones*, the humor springs from the fact that Professor Potts, a pioneer paleontologist, puts together the dinosaur bones he's unearthed in a variety of ways. In the text, he rejects each construction on the ground that no such animal could possibly have existed. But we see from the illustrations that they're actually a triceratops, a brontosaurus, and Tyrannosaurus Rex. Carol Carrick conveyed this necessary information about the professor's mistakes in marginal notes.

Even when explanations like the above are required to make your intentions as an author perfectly clear, try to keep them as short as possible. You don't want to put off editors by making them feel you doubt their ability to visualize the text. Nor do you want to inhibit the imagination of an illustrator by giving him or her overly detailed instructions.

Picture book authors frequently ask another question: "Should I go a step further and get an artist friend to make sample illustrations for my story before I submit it to a publisher?" Emphatically, "No." Unless your friend is a professional illustrator and you've worked jointly on the project from its inception, you'll be far better off letting your story speak for itself. Once you've sold the manuscript, the editor and art director will be responsible for finding the best possible illustrator for the book.

## The author-illustrator

But what if you are the illustrator as well as the author, as many picture book creators are today? Then, of course, you'll think in terms of a dummy from the very start and sketch in your ideas for illustrations. Some artists do very loose dummy sketches, others make detailed drawings or paintings that could almost serve as finished art. There's no set rule about this; it all depends on how the particular artist prefers to work, and most editors and art directors are comfortable with either approach.

Whether the dummy is loose or detailed, it's also a good idea to do at least two or three sample illustrations to show editors and art directors how you intend the finished book to look. Don't send out the actual samples when you submit the manuscript, however; there's too much danger that they'll be damaged in handling or become dog-eared. Enclose good color photographs or photocopies of the samples instead, and submit them with a clear photocopy of the dummy—not the original. In an accompanying note, you can say you'll be happy to send the originals if the editor is seriously interested in the project.

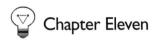 Chapter Eleven

# To Rhyme or Not to Rhyme?

**M**any novice picture book authors are troubled by a hard-to-decide question when they sit down at their computers: Should I write my story in prose or verse? Rightly or wrongly, a sizable number choose the latter course. Of the thousands of picture book submissions that publishers receive in any given year, probably a quarter to a third are written in verse.

Some are collections of original poems that the authors hope to see published in anthology form with colorful illustrations. Unfortunately, the market for such picture book anthologies is extremely limited unless (a) the author already has an established reputation as a children's poet, or (b) the poems center on a popular theme, like holidays or the seasons, and are of truly exceptional quality.

Many authors decide to write their picture book manuscripts, both fantasies and realistic stories, in verse form. The decision probably stems from the authors' observation of their target audience. For almost from babyhood, and certainly from the time they first hear "Mother Goose," children everywhere respond to the rhythms, repeated patterns, and rhyme schemes of poetry.

Theodor Geisel (Dr. Seuss) was well aware of this when he wrote *The Cat in the Hat* and his other tremendously popular stories in lilting couplets that use the simplest words. After observing a child's delighted reaction to one of

Seuss's books, it's easy to understand why an aspiring writer for children might decide to try his or her hand at something similar. It looks so easy. What these people fail to realize is that writing good poetry in any form is extremely difficult, and writing a complete story in verse is probably the most difficult task of all.

It can be done. Eve Bunting, in her picture book *Scary, Scary Halloween*, sets the tone and style of the entire story with this opening stanza:

> I peer outside, there's something there
> That makes me shiver, spikes my hair.
> It must be Halloween.

Note how the author uses very simple language, then injects an unusual verb in the phrase "spikes my hair." That sort of verbal play is not only permitted but desirable in poetry.

Note, too, how the stanza, in just seventeen words, sets up a dramatic situation, generates suspense, and creates a vivid scene for an artist to illustrate. That's what the beginning of every picture book text, whether written in poetry or prose, should ideally achieve. But few accomplish it as swiftly and sparingly as does *Scary, Scary Halloween*. That's probably because Eve Bunting understands that the verse form, when handled deftly, requires an author to write in a more compressed and economical style.

Verse also allows an author to reach for dramatic effects in language that might seem overdone if written in prose. Here's an example from a later passage in *Scary, Scary Halloween*.

> Thunder, thunder up above!
> "What is it, Mother?" "Shh, my love!
> It's just the thump of creature feet,
> A creature in a winding sheet,

His claws are dragging on the floor.
He's crashing, smashing at the door!"
"Will he find us here, below?"
"Shh, my love, I cannot know."

To justify such heightened language, an author needs
a powerful dramatic situation at the core of the story.
*Scary, Scary Halloween* has such a situation: It's a fantasy
about four pairs of green eyes that watch a parade of fearsome creatures go past the house where they're hiding
under the porch. Only at the end, as we said earlier, does
the author confirm what bright youngsters will have
guessed all along: that the creatures are Halloween trick-
or-treaters, and the green eyes belong to a mother cat and
her three kittens.

But a larger-than-life situation is not always necessary.
The casual lyrics of a Dorothy Parker or an Ogden Nash
make their points neatly and wittily even as they tell a story.
And the same effect can be achieved in a picture book text
for children. Beatrice Schenk de Regniers has done it in
many books, including *So Many Cats.* Just look at (and read
aloud) these lines from the latter story:

We had a cat—
an Only Cat
She was a sad
and lonely cat.
So when a very hungry cat
came making a great din,
meowing, mewing
scratching at our door,
we thought
this could be the very cat
to make our cat a happy cat,
and so we let her in—

little knowing we were getting more
than we had
bargained
for.

The tone here is so natural and conversational that you may not even be conscious that the author is writing in verse until you suddenly become aware of the clever internal rhyme scheme. The text also does much more than simply display her skill as a poet. It immediately characterizes the unnamed child narrator as a warm, perceptive cat-lover with a dry sense of humor. And, like *Scary, Scary Halloween* and all good picture book texts, it offers one opportunity after another for lively, active illustrations.

## Practical steps

It's instructive for an aspiring writer of stories in verse to read about successful books like these two. But what other practical steps can you take to help you save time and avoid making mistakes when you sit down to write your own stories? Here are a few suggestions:

1. To find out what verse stories are being published for children today, go to the children's department of your local library or to a good children's bookstore and ask for a list of recommended titles. Analyze the books, as we've done with *Scary, Scary Halloween* and *So Many Cats*, to see how the authors achieve their effects. No doubt you'll discover some approaches and techniques that you can apply to your own writing.

2. After examining a wide variety of books, you may decide your poetic skills are rusty and need sharpening. Perhaps you wrote a lot of poetry in high school and college, but that was a long time ago. If so, it may be worthwhile for you to take a course in poetry writing at your local college,

university, or adult education center. What you learn about different verse forms and how to write them will extend your poetic range and enable you to tell your story in more than just rhyming couplets.

3. Use whatever poetic form you select to help you tell your story more dramatically or humorously. In an effort to maintain a rhyming scheme, don't get so involved in the form itself that every other element—characterization, plot, etc.—is sacrificed to it. Too many verse stories by beginning authors run on to 10 or 12 pages because the author has become more concerned with maintaining a poetic pattern than with telling the story.

It's important to remember that a story in verse should observe the same rules as any other picture book text. If it's aimed at quite young children, like *Scary, Scary Halloween*, it should be no more than two or three double-spaced manuscript pages. If it's intended for a slightly older audience of, say, five-to-eight-year-olds, like *So Many Cats*, it can be as long as five or six manuscript pages.

Whatever the length, it should—like other picture books—have characters that the reader can care about, a strong plot with a beginning, middle, and end, and if possible, a final surprise twist at the end. No restless youngsters are going to sit still for rhythm and rhyme if there's nothing else in the story to hold their attention.

## Lyrical, *speakable* prose

Maybe, after deciding to write your story in verse and doing several drafts of it, you become discouraged. The rhymes seem forced, and you feel as if you're losing your grip on the story line. What should you do? Stop work on the story and put it in a drawer until inspiration strikes again? Or try a different approach?

The latter course would probably be the best. For, as

many successful authors have discovered, stories for children can be rhythmic without being written in verse. The trick is to write them in lyrical prose—and the result is often more effective.

What exactly is lyrical prose? It's prose that incorporates many of the characteristics of poetry for children, including rhythm, repetition, and the use of unusual, vivid words to add flavor to the text. Most important of all, it's *speakable*. In an era when more and more parents are reading aloud to their children from the time they're babies, the speakability of a picture book story has become even more essential than it was in the past.

Let's look at some good examples of lyrical, speakable prose. Here's one from the opening of *The Half-Birthday Party* by Charlotte Pomerantz:

> One day, when Daniel's sister Katie
> was six months old,
> She stood for the first time.
> She took hold of a table leg
> and pulled herself up.
> "Daddy, Mommy, come quick," said Daniel.
> "Katie is standing."
>
> That evening, Daniel decided
> to give Katie a half-birthday party.
> He sent an invitation to Lily,
> his friend across the hall.
> And one to Grandma and Mr. Bangs,
> who always came to parties with her.
> The invitation read:
>
> My sister Katie is six months old.
> Please come to her half-birthday party
> on Sunday afternoon at 3 o'clock.

And bring half a present.

Daniel

P. S. You have to tell a whole story
about the half present.

In this relatively brief passage, the author accomplishes
a great deal. She gets the story moving right away by
establishing Daniel's pride in his little sister when she
stands for the first time, and his idea for the half-birthday
party. And she does it in simple but rhythmic prose. Try
reading the passage aloud and you'll see just how speakable
it is.

Lyrical prose can be used to achieve many different
kinds of effects. Carol Carrick employs it in her picture story
book, *Dark and Full of Secrets*, to create a mood of forebod-
ing and suspense. Here's how the story begins:

Early morning mist rose from the pond like
steam from a witch's brew. Christopher's father
held the canoe steady. Just as Christopher was
climbing in, his dog Ben jumped in with him,
making the boat rock.

"Ben!" Christopher yelled, pushing the dog
out.

"Home, Ben! Go home!" his father ordered,
pointing toward the house. Ben slunk away.

"Today will be a scorcher," Christopher's father
said as they pushed off. "A good day for swimming."

"I don't like to go in the pond," said
Christopher. "There are things in there, and the
bottom is all mucky."

It wasn't that Christopher didn't like swimming.

In the ocean the waves rose green like glass and,
when they broke over him, the sudsy foam made
him tingle. But the pond was dark and full of secrets.

Note how the author, although writing in prose, weaves
in poetic imagery to add color to her language. Instead of
simply stating "Early morning mist rose from the pond" and
leaving it at that, she goes on to say that it rose "like steam
from a witch's brew." And see how she builds a rhythmic
flow in the last paragraph of the passage, culminating in the
description of the pond as being "dark and full of secrets."
This may be prose, but it hooks a reader with all the force
and imagination of poetry.

## "Speakability" tests

Whether you're writing lyrical prose or actual poetry, how
can you test your own writing to make sure it's as imaginative—and "speakable"—as possible? Here are some ideas
that have worked well for other authors, and should work
for you, too.

1. Go over the completed draft of your manuscript and
look critically at all the images you've used. Are they fresh or
flat? If you decide that too many of them fall in the second
category, try to think of better ones. Don't strain for an
effect, but at the same time don't miss a chance to leave an
impression on the reader, either.

2. Reread your story and ask yourself the following questions: Does the writing flow smoothly from one sentence and
paragraph to another, with breaks in the rhythm here and
there when something exciting or funny happens? Or does it
contain too many stiff and awkward stretches?

If you're unsure about the latter, try reading the story
aloud, either to yourself or to a sympathetic listener. If you

still have difficulty judging whether the text speaks well or not, record it and play back the tape. As you listen, mark those places in the manuscript that seem jerky, or that don't make their points as clearly and sharply as you would like. Those are the sections that you should revise and polish before you send the manuscript to a publisher.

 Chapter Twelve

# From Submission to Contract

At last, after long hours of hard work at your desk, you've completed your picture book, nonfiction proposal, or novel. Print out a copy, then let it sit for a few days or a week before you read it through. That pause should enable you to see the manuscript more objectively. Then you can rework any passages that seem awkward or unclear, and also correct typos the spell check on your computer failed to catch. Once all these final changes are in place, and you've made several copies of the revised version, your manuscript will be ready to go out into the world. What's the best way to go about this?

Before submitting their manuscripts to publishers, some authors wonder if they should protect their ownership of the material by copyrighting the manuscripts as unpublished works with the Register of Copyrights at the Library of Congress in Washington, D.C. In my opinion, this is an unnecessary step and expense. Under the 1978 Copyright Act, all "original works of authorship" have automatic copyright protection from the moment they are "fixed in any tangible medium of expression." This protection lasts for the author's lifetime, plus 50 years. After a book is published, it becomes the publisher's responsibility to copyright it as a published work. In the case of most children's books, the copyright for the text is taken out in the author's name.

Now back to the submission process. Ideally you should

have done the necessary homework beforehand so that as soon as the manuscript is finished you can send it off to the first publishing house on your list. But whether you do it in advance or after the manuscript is in final form, here are the steps you should take in order to handle the submission process as efficiently—and effectively—as possible.

## The submission process

1. To begin with, you'll need to get a sense of the children's book market. A good way to start is by studying the current catalogues of children's book publishers. You can probably find them in the children's department of your local library—just ask the librarian where they're kept. Look, too, at the publishers' seasonal list ads that appear in trade magazines such as *Publishers Weekly* and *School Library Journal*. Those in the former publication can be found in the special children's book issues that come out in February to announce spring titles and in July to herald the new fall books.

2. When you have a feel for the different publishing houses and what types of books they do, you'll have a much better idea of which houses might be interested in your manuscript. But before packing up your material and sending it off to one of them, you'll need to do more research in order to find the answer to another crucial question: *Is the publisher open to unsolicited submissions that come direct from an author?*

Once upon a time all children's book publishers considered direct submissions, but those days are long gone. Now almost half the publishers have stopped reading unsolicited manuscripts. The main reason for this change in policy can be put into two words: expense reduction. Studies by the business departments at many publishing houses show that screening thousands of direct submissions is simply not cost-effective. The small number of publishable manuscripts the readers turn up does not justify the large number of staff hours spent in processing them . . . or so the business people say.

Editors often feel otherwise. At Clarion Books, for example, many of the firm's most respected and successful writers have emerged from the so-called slush pile of unsolicited manuscripts, and the same is true at other houses. But it's hard to argue with statistics from a business department when it decides to wield a budgetary ax against expenses.

3. What can writers do to circumvent a publisher's policy not to accept unsolicited submissions? There are several constructive steps you can take. If you meet an editor at a writers' conference, try to introduce yourself and mention the type of material you write. Having met you, the editor may make an exception and agree to read your manuscript, even though his or her publishing house has a policy of not reading unsolicited manuscripts. Or the editor may say "no" to a complete manuscript, but be willing to take a look at a partial manuscript or a query from you.

4. You can't count on such chance encounters, however. *A more practical way to bring your manuscript to an editor's attention is to study carefully up-to-date market listings.* Some of the most comprehensive are those found in *Book Markets for Children's Writers* and *Magazine Markets for Children's Writers*, both issued by the Institute of Children's Literature, 93 Long Ridge Road, West Redding, CT 06896-1124. www.WritersBookstore.com

Another excellent marketing resource is the bimonthly *Bulletin* of the Society of Children's Book Writers and Illustrators. The Society, located at 8271 Beverly Boulevard, Los Angeles, CA 90048, has almost 20,000 members worldwide, and is the largest American organization devoted solely to the needs and interests of children's book authors and illustrators. Writers can join the Society as associate members before they have had anything published and receive its *Bulletin*, as well as its annual, updated lists of children's book publishers, their current submission policies, and the names of their editors and art directors.

5. As you study the possible markets for your work, you may find that while one publisher has slammed the door shut on unsolicited submissions, another has opened it. *Keep an eye out especially for new imprints and what their special requirements are*; for example, some may plan to publish only easy readers, others only multicultural books. Usually, these new imprints are open to direct submissions from writers, at least at first, because they're in the process of building their lists.

Whether the publishers are new or long-established, they often add restrictions to their policy statements that you'll need to pay close attention to. Some may say that the only complete manuscripts they're willing to consider are those for picture books. With all nonfiction projects, and all fiction manuscripts of more than, say, 25 pages, they prefer to see query letters first. Other publishers may say that they want to see outlines and two or three sample chapters of novels. (Few publishers ask for a query letter or outline on a picture book unless it's part of a proposed board book series; the query letter might be longer than the actual text!)

## Fiction query letters

Query letters for fiction manuscripts are similar in many ways to those for nonfiction projects that were discussed in Chapter 2. But there are some major differences also. Here are a few tips on how to write effective fiction queries:

1. In the opening paragraph, tell what category the story falls into—mystery, adventure, humorous, animal, etc.—give the title, and say what age group it's aimed at.

2. Go on to provide some idea of the story's content. This needn't be a complete, detailed synopsis of the plot; in

fact, it probably shouldn't be. But it should convey who the main character is, what he or she is striving for, some of the obstacles—scary or funny—that have to be overcome along the way, and whether or not the character succeeds in the end.

3. Include a rundown of your publishing credits, high-lighting those that are especially relevant to your new manu-script; for example, previous novels (and publishers) or short stories in a similar vein that have appeared in children's magazines.

If you don't have any credits yet, say that, too. The editor won't hold it against you, since he knows that everyone has to start somewhere.

4. End the letter with a simple question: "Would you be interested in seeing the outline and sample chapters of my novel, or the complete manuscript?"

If possible, try to confine your query letter to one, or at most two, single-spaced typewritten pages. And be sure to include a self-addressed, stamped envelope when you mail it off to an editor.

5. Make copies of your query letters and use them to start a submission file on your book. Some authors also like to maintain a computer or file card record on each of their manuscripts, with entries of when and to whom it was sent out and when it came back, but I personally find that a file folder is enough. Besides hard copies of your own letters, you should also keep every editorial response you get to the manuscript. In this way, you'll have a complete submission history of the project in case you need to refer to it at some later date.

*One final word about query letters: Most children's book editors don't mind receiving a simultaneous query letter, that is, one being sent to several other editors at the same time.*

6. When an editor responds favorably to your query, it's time to get the manuscript ready to mail. If you receive more

than one positive response, send the manuscript to the publisher you prefer and hold the other letters for future follow-up in case the first publisher declines it.

## Cover letters

Should you write a cover letter to accompany the manuscript? Some say it's better to let the material speak for itself, but I happen to like cover letters, and so do many other editors. They're essential when a manuscript is being submitted at the editor's invitation, for they'll remind the editor of your original query, which is probably being held in a "pending" file. They also serve a useful purpose if they accompany a direct submission like a picture book story . . . as long as they're brief and to the point.

Since the editor-author relationship is a highly personal one, you can make use of the cover letter to introduce yourself to the editor as a literate, caring human being. Besides giving the title and category of your manuscript in the first sentence, you can go on to say in a few carefully chosen words what impelled you to write it, and then you can list your relevant writing credits if you have some.

1. Whether or not you include a cover letter, *you should pack your manuscript carefully before sending it off.* As an editor I'm constantly surprised by the authors who simply fold up their picture book manuscripts and stick them into #10 envelopes or put heavy rubber bands around the pages of their novels and then shove them into mailers. Such treatment virtually guarantees that the manuscript will arrive at the publisher's office in a torn or disheveled condition. Why not put your manuscript into a file folder or, in the case of a novel, two folders or a cardboard box before mailing it? That won't add much to the weight of the package, and your submission will make a much better impression when it's opened in the editor's office.

2. If you want the editor to acknowledge receipt of the

manuscript, enclose a stamped, self-addressed postcard with a line for the editorial department to fill in, saying they received the manuscript on such-and-such a date. In any case, be sure to enclose a stamped, self-addressed envelope or mailer (same size as you used for submission) for the return of the manuscript if it doesn't meet the editor's needs.

## How long to wait?

You've mailed off your manuscript, and within a week or so you get back the acknowledgment card stating that it arrived at the publisher's office. Then you wait. You realize the editor needs time to read and evaluate your submission, but as the weeks and sometimes months go by, you gradually lose patience. *What's a reasonable waiting time for a decision?* you wonder. *And what if anything can be done to hasten the process?*

Because most editorial staffs are small, it usually takes at least four to eight weeks to evaluate a picture book manuscript or nonfiction proposal, and six weeks to three months for a longer fiction manuscript. Whether the wait is shorter or longer generally depends on how many readings the manuscript is given.

If these time periods have passed and you haven't heard from the publisher, write a letter of inquiry asking if the manuscript is still being considered. Enclose another stamped, self-addressed postcard for the editor's reply. (An email letter would be faster, but most publishers prefer to reserve their email correspondence for projects in the works and interoffice communications.)

Wait several more weeks, and if the publisher hasn't replied, telephone the editorial department and ask about the status of your manuscript. Then, if you still don't receive a satisfactory response to your inquiries, write the editor a polite note stating that since you haven't heard anything you've decided to withdraw your manuscript from consideration in order to submit it elsewhere. Send the note by certified mail, with a return receipt requested.

## What about multiple submissions?

If you've been burned several times by long delays, you may decide to try another tack—submitting your manuscript to several publishers simultaneously. There was a time when I argued against multiple submissions as they're called, but no longer. I still believe that diligent followup on an exclusive submission is the ideal policy to pursue. But after hearing of instances where writers have waited anywhere from six months to three years for decisions, I've decided that the multiple submission route may be the only way to go, especially if you're just starting out. *And I don't think you need to tell publishers it is a multiple submission if you feel that would decrease your chances of getting a full reading.*

Of course, even when you submit to several publishers simultaneously you'll probably experience delays and have to follow up on your manuscript with letters and phone calls. But at least you'll have the satisfaction of knowing five or six different houses are considering the manuscript, and not just one. In the meantime, you should make up a second list of publishers to whom you can submit the project in case one or more of your first choices declines it. This will help to keep your spirits up—and the manuscript in play—until you get an affirmative response.

Multiple submissions can lead to problems. What would you do, for instance, if two publishers offered you a contract at the same time? I'd choose the house and editor you'd prefer to publish with, and tell the second editor that you appreciate his or her offer but have had a better one else-where. You should also inform the other publishers to whom you submitted the manuscript that it has been sold. That way, they won't invest any more time and money in considering it.

There are exceptions to this multiple submission policy. For example, once you've established an ongoing relationship with an editor, you should give that person an *exclusive* look at a new manuscript before showing it to other editors. If for some reason your editor turns down the project, then you can take the multiple submission route again. But let's hope that won't be necessary, and the first editor will come through with a contract!

## Should I get an agent?

If you feel frustrated as ever more publishers stop considering unsolicited submissions, you may decide it's time to get a literary agent to represent you. That's sometimes easier said than done, however. With increasing numbers of writers seeking their services, agents have become more selective. It's still possible to connect with a good agent, though. Here are some suggestions of how to go about it.

1. You can find many agents for children's material listed in *Literary Marketplace* and other reference sources such as the lists issued by the Society of Children's Book Writers and Illustrators and the Association of Authors' Representatives. After studying these sources, make up your own list of possible agents. Don't rule out the large, well-known agencies. Their top agents may not be taking on any neophytes, but often these agencies have young agents on staff who are trying to build client lists. One of these start-up agents may have room for you.

Don't overlook agents with offices outside of New York City, either. Many professionals have relocated away from New York in recent years and established small businesses of their own. They're often more open to talented beginners, and have more time to devote to promoting their work.

2. With your list in hand, develop a query letter to send to the agents. In the letter, you should introduce yourself and your writing, and ask the agents if they'd be willing to read

samples of your work. Try to limit the letter to one page, single-spaced.

Let's say you mail out query letters to 15 agents and get four positive responses. Several of these may tell you exactly what the agents want to see in the way of sample material—a single picture book text, a proposal for a nonfiction book, or three chapters and the outline of a novel. Take them at their word, and send no more—or less—than they requested.

If the agents do not specify the amount of material they're willing to read, use your best judgment in putting together a selection of your writings. Send only examples of what you consider to be your best work, and don't send too much material. You don't want to overwhelm the agent.

As you pursue the search for an agent, don't stop submitting manuscripts on your own. Due to their small staffs, agents may take as long to reply as editors do . . . maybe longer. In the meantime, you shouldn't put your writing career on hold.

3. After evaluating your material, perhaps two of the four interested agents will eventually write to say they'd be happy to represent you. Now it's time for you to ask the two agents a few questions about their backgrounds and ways of working:

(a) Have they had children's book publishing experience, and have they worked with the leading editors in the field?

(b) Who are some of the other children's authors they represent?

(c) What commission will the agents take from the proceeds of your book? The standard percentage used to be 10% of all moneys received, but as the costs of doing business have risen, many agents now charge 15% or even 20% for their services.

(d) Lastly, what formal arrangements, if any, do the agents make with their clients? Some agents require writers to sign a one- or two-year contract with them. But many others—including some of the best—operate on the basis of a handshake agreement. If you're satisfied with each other's performance, fine; if not, you're both free to part company.

Once you have answers to these questions, you should be able to make an intelligent choice between the two interested agents. And, with your agent's help, you'll be able to get past those editorial doors that have been closed to you up till now.

## Just what *is* the editor saying?

Whether you submit your manuscripts through an agent or on your own, the time will come when you'll hear from an editor. The response may be anything from an outright rejection to a letter offering various degrees of encouragement. Whatever form the response takes, it may confuse more than it enlightens and leave you asking, "Just what *is* the editor saying?" Here is a brief guide to the most common types of letters editors write when returning a manuscript, and what each type usually means.

1. *The printed form rejection slip.* This is just what it seems—a flat rejection. The editor simply couldn't use your manuscript, and with five thousand or more submissions crowding into his or her office each year, neither he nor anyone on the staff had the time to write you a personal letter.

2. Sometimes, though, you'll find a *handwritten note scrawled at the bottom of the rejection slip*—"Nice touches of humor (or suspense or drama). Try us again." This probably means that the editor or his first reader liked some things about your manuscript and is inviting you to make other submissions. If you get such a note, take the person who wrote it at his word and send him another manuscript.

3. Perhaps you'll get a *similarly encouraging personal letter, signed by the editor*, in which he comments briefly on your manuscript, wishes you luck in placing it elsewhere, and invites you to submit more material. This means that the editor himself read your manuscript and saw something in it.

While a letter like this is far from an acceptance, it shouldn't be dismissed either, for no busy editor takes the time to write such a note unless he sees promise in an author's work.

4. Then there's the much longer letter that you may get in which *the editor goes into detail about what he likes and doesn't like in the manuscript*, makes specific suggestions for improving it, and says that he'll be happy to read the manuscript again if you decide to revise it. Such a letter means exactly what it says—that the editor is serious about your manuscript and thinks it may find a place on his list if you correct its weaknesses through revision.

*How should you respond to such a letter?* To begin with, you shouldn't ignore it or set it aside, even though the idea of getting back into the manuscript and making extensive changes may seem daunting. Next, you should evaluate the editor's suggestions carefully, decide if you agree with them, and then write the editor a letter. Thank him for taking an interest in your manuscript, and then go on to tell him your reactions to his suggestions. Perhaps you disagree with some of them; if so, be direct about it and explain your reasons. On the other hand, his comments may have sparked ideas for different ways to solve the problems in the manuscript. Share these with him; it will help to get an author-editor discussion going.

If you've decided you want to revise the manuscript, let the editor know how long you think the revision will take you to do. Don't feel you have to get the manuscript back to him within a week. If he's genuinely interested in your material—and you have to assume he is—he won't forget it so quickly. And he'll have more respect for you as an author if he senses you'll spend the time needed to think through the revisions instead of making them hastily and rushing the manuscript back to him.

Some authors have told me that they're reluctant to

make major revisions on speculation without any assurance that they'll eventually get a contract for the manuscript. Of course that has to be an individual decision, and it can be especially difficult for an established author who's used to receiving a contract before revisions. But for a beginning author, I believe it's generally worth the gamble, and I can speak from personal experience in this regard. For my first book, *The Scarecrow Book*, my collaborator Dale Ferguson and I did three sets of sample material before the editor was convinced the project deserved a contract. Looking back now, I'm glad we did, for the process helped us sharpen the focus of the book.

In my capacity as editor, I asked Mary Downing Hahn for four revisions of her first novel, *The Sara Summer*, before we decided the story would make a successful book. The author said she learned a lot about both writing and editing from this experience and I certainly gained a greater respect for her as an author. Moreover, it led to an ongoing editor-author relationship, as she and I worked together on many more novels—none of which required as many revisions as *The Sara Summer*.

Finally, after who knows how many submissions and perhaps as many revisions, there comes that exciting day when you open a new letter from the editor and read: "We're happy to tell you that your manuscript seems in solid shape now and we would like to contract it for publication."

After reveling in unabashed euphoria for a while, and calling your husband, wife, mother, or best friend to tell them the exciting news, you sit down to read the contract terms outlined in the rest of the letter. You may find some of these terms hard to understand—many first-time authors do. But the key provisions in a standard book contract really aren't that difficult to grasp, as we'll see in the next chapter.

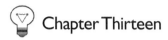 Chapter Thirteen

# From Contract to Publication—and Beyond

Some publishers' contracts are long, others are shorter, but in either case most of the pages are filled with what are known in the trade as "boilerplate clauses." These concern such things as the author's responsibility to protect the publisher from a libel suit, what will happen if the author fails to deliver the manuscript or the publisher fails to publish it, and how the author can regain his rights in the work if the book goes out of print.

If you have an agent, he will negotiate the contract with the publisher and explain any confusing terms or clauses to you. An author who doesn't have an agent may think he should have a lawyer look over the contract for him. Since few lawyers are experienced in literary and copyright law, they are not likely to be too helpful. In most instances, you'll probably be better off if you read the contract carefully yourself, make a list of those points that aren't clear, and discuss them with your editor or someone in the publisher's contract department. In the meantime, here are the key points you should look for first in any contract:

## How you will be paid for your material

Most children's book publishers offer an advance against royalties, but some may offer you a flat fee. In the latter arrangement, you'll be paid a certain amount for all rights to your material, and will receive no further income from it, no matter how many copies the book sells. Established authors usually refuse to accept flat-fee contracts, but if you're just starting out and have tried to place the manuscript at a number of houses, you may feel that it's more important to get it published than to hold out for a royalty contract. In any case, there's no harm in asking the publisher if there's a possibility of getting a royalty on the book when sales reach a certain point . . . say, 3% of the list price after 10,000 copies have been sold. The worst the publisher can say is "No."

If you're offered an advance against royalties, the size of the advance will depend on what type of book your project is.

In recent years, the typical hardcover advance on a picture book text by a new author was in the neighborhood of $3,000-$4,000, while the advance on a first novel ranged from $4,000-$6,000. Advances have gradually risen along with hardcover book prices and the economy in general, so it's safe to assume that they'll continue to rise in the future.

Royalties also depend on the nature of the book. The customary royalty for a new author is 10% of the book's catalogue list price, but in the case of a picture book the author shares this royalty with the illustrator, each of them receiving 5%. On nonfiction photo essays, the royalty is usually divided 50/50 between the author and photographer. And if a novel or nonfiction project requires some illustrations, the author may be asked to take a royalty of 7% or 8% so that the illustrator can be given a 2% or 3% royalty. As a consequence, only the author of an unillustrated novel can be pretty sure of getting the full 10% royalty.

Some publishers base the author's royalty on the net amount the book brings in after discount rather than the list price. A bit of arithmetic will show that a net royalty contract is much less advantageous to the author. Say the book carries a retail or list price of $14.00, and your royalty is 10% of list; that means you'll be earning $1.40 on each copy sold. However, if your royalty is 10% of net, and the average discount on the book to retailers and wholesalers is 40% or 50%, you'll receive only $.84 or $.70 per copy sold.

You may grumble about this, but you're not likely to budge a net royalty publisher from his position, especially if you're a new author with no sales track record. As with flat fee contracts, you'll have to base your decision on whether or not to accept a net royalty on how enthusiastic you feel about the particular publisher, and whether you think it's the best home you can find for your manuscript.

Established author friends may tell you that they're receiving a sliding scale royalty on their books and urge you to ask your publisher for the same. You can ask, but you'll almost certainly be turned down, for no author is given a sliding scale until he's proven his mettle by delivering a string of successful books. What exactly is a sliding scale royalty? Basically it's an increase in the royalty rate from 10% to 12½% of the list price on novels or, in the case of picture books and photo essays, from 5% to 6¼%, with the rise occurring after a certain number of copies of the book have been sold. This breaking point may be as low as 7,500 copies in the case of a novel or as high as 15,000 copies on a full-color picture book, where the publisher's initial production costs are much steeper.

Whether you have a standard royalty or a sliding scale contract, the book will have to sell enough copies to earn back the initial advance before you get any additional royalties.

Using a $14.00 list price again, and assuming that the book is a novel for which you received an advance of $5000 against a royalty of 10%, your break-even point on the book would be sales of approximately 3,500 copies. In the case of a first book, that point probably won't be reached until six months or more after the book's publication. On all sales after that, you'll receive your $1.40 royalty per book.

Most publishers compute and pay royalties twice a year on sales in the preceding six months, which is why I often say to authors that books are like bonds, and royalty checks like interest payments. Only a few children's book authors and illustrators get rich from their work, but those who produce a steady stream of successful titles can, in time, make a comfortable income.

## Subsidiary rights

The next clauses you should look for in a royalty contract are those that tell you *what percentage you will receive of the income from subsidiary rights.* These rights include the possible sale of your book to a book club, a paperback reprinter, a foreign publisher, a textbook anthology, a filmstrip or audiotape producer, and in the case of a few junior novels, a television or movie producer. There are also electronic rights, which promise to play an increasingly important role in the juvenile rights picture.

Although subsidiary rights deals in the children's book field rarely command the spectacular advances that make news in adult publishing, some children's book authors—especially of fiction—earn hefty amounts of money from the sale of subsidiary rights in their books.

If you have an agent, he will handle the foreign and audio-visual rights in your book, while the publisher takes care of domestic book clubs and paperback reprinters. If you don't have an agent, the publisher will be responsible for selling all of the subsidiary rights in the property, often with the aid of agents abroad. Trust him to do the best job he can with the book; not only does he have the necessary expertise, but he also stands to make a profit on each sale.

The division of subsidiary rights income between author and publisher varies somewhat from house to house, but here are some standard splits against which you can compare those in your contract:

> (a) *Book clubs, paperback reprints, and sales to textbook publishers:* 50% to the author, 50% to the publisher (or, in the case of a picture book, 25% to the author and 25% to the illustrator).
> (b) *Foreign sales:* 75% to the author and 25% to the publisher (or, with a picture book, 37½% to the author and 37½% to the illustrator).
> (c) *Film rights:* 80% or 90% to the author; 10% or 20% to the publisher. (Since film rights are usually sold only on novels, which are not illustrated, the author generally receives the entire share.)

Once you've established a firm reputation with a publisher, you may be able to negotiate some of these percentages upward, especially those covering foreign and film rights. But, along with the advance and the royalty rate on the publisher's edition, the subsidiary rights percentages in most first book contracts are not negotiable.

## The option clause

This clause gives the publisher the right of first refusal on your next children's book manuscript, and sometimes on your next two manuscripts. Most editors insist that first-time authors agree to the inclusion of an option clause in the contract, and actually, I feel it's to the author's advantage, since it confirms the publisher's ongoing interest in the author's work. However, once an author becomes established and perhaps begins to publish with more than one house, he generally asks that the option be struck out of his contracts.

The clause isn't all that restrictive in any case. If an author is terribly unhappy with an editor or publisher, he can always pull an old manuscript out of the drawer, submit it as his next project, and rejoice in being a free agent again when the manuscript is rejected.

## The clause regarding permissions

If you quote from published material in your manuscript, you should pay special attention to the clause—standard in most contracts—that states you are responsible for obtaining permission to reprint these extracts in your book and paying any fees that may be involved. Written permission is usually required only for passages of more than 50 words from books or magazines published within the past 50 years or so, but if you're in any doubt as to whether you need to get clearance, it's best to write to the permissions departments of the publishers in question.

In my experience, the steepest fees are often charged for the use of lines from contemporary song lyrics and poems by well-known present-day authors. If these, and other, permissions fees seem onerous to you, you may decide to paraphrase the quotations involved or even omit them from your manuscript.

## On to publication

Once the contract has been negotiated and signed, and you've received your advance, what happens next? And what role will you be expected to play in the development of the book?

At some point you're sure to receive a request from the editorial or publicity department for biographical information and a photograph. Take your time with this, and answer the publisher's questions as fully as possible. He'll especially welcome anecdotes about your background and where you got the idea for the book that can be woven into the jacket copy. Provide him also with a photograph that does you justice; as an editor, I know how disappointing it is when a new author sends in an out-of-focus snapshot that could never be used on the jacket or in any other publicity material.

On some biographical questionnaires there's space for the author to write a brief description of his book. Try to make this summary as lively and intriguing as you can, for the editor may well use it—or parts of it—on the front jacket flap of the book or in the announcement catalogue.

On a novel or nonfiction book, the editor will send you the copyeditor's queries to go over and answer. These generally concern minor matters of styling and punctuation consistency, but sometimes the copyeditor will ask you to clarify a point or rewrite a confusing passage. As with any revision suggestions, you should examine the pages in question, try to see what the copyeditor is getting at, and go along with all of his suggestions that seem reasonable. For his aim, like yours, is to make the book as good as it can be.

If you've written a picture book, the editor may, as a courtesy, show you samples of the illustrator's work or even a copy of the dummy to check for accuracy of detail. But you won't have approval of the illustrator, nor will you or any author have approval of the jacket design for your book. Those creative decisions are made by the editor and the art director, and at many houses, members of the marketing department staff have a say in them also.

After the manuscript has been copyedited and designed, the next stage in any book is galley or page proofs. These are uncorrected proofs of the text. For a picture book, there may be only one sheet; for a teenage novel as many as 150. In any case, you'll receive a set to read, correct, and return to the publisher. A professional proofreader and probably the editor will be reading them, too, and the aim of all these readings is to catch as many typographical errors as possible.

Some authors, when they go over the proofs, suddenly

decide they'd like to rewrite entire passages of their books. It's wise to restrain such impulses and limit yourself to a few spots that, for one reason or another, you feel should be polished or clarified. If you don't restrain yourself your editor will, for it costs a great deal to reset large chunks of type (and some contracts call for all or part of these costs to be charged to the author).

Following the proofs come repros and other production stages that you probably won't be involved in. Then the book will be presented to the house's sales representatives at the seasonal sales conference. Most children's book departments participate in two of these conferences each year, one in March or April at which the new titles to be published in the fall are described enthusiastically by the editor, and another in November or December at which all the spring titles are introduced.

Jacket proofs of the new books are prepared for these conferences so the sales reps will have something to show their customers, and proofs of the interiors of picture books and some heavily illustrated nonfiction books are handed out also. After the conference, your editor will probably send you the jacket proof for your book, or complete proofs— called "folded and gathered sheets"—of your picture book, and then it'll be time for oo-ing and ah-ing. (But if you or the editor catch a typo on the jacket, or in the picture book, you'll still be able to correct it.)

Finally, several months after the sales conference in most instances, the great day arrives when you receive the first bound copy of your book in the mail. It will be followed shortly by your other free author's copies, generally 15 or 20 in all, depending on the number specified in your contract. Picture book authors may get fewer free copies because, like the royalty, these are usually divided with the illustrator. But all authors and illustrators receive a discount on additional copies of the book that they wish to purchase.

## Waiting for reviews

Now comes the exciting—and scary—time of waiting for reviews of the book. The most influential are not, as you might suppose, the ones that run in major national consumer publications, such as the *New York Times Book Review*. Instead, they're those that appear in five literary and review periodicals, unknown to most laymen, but held in high esteem by public and school librarians. The five periodicals are:

> *School Library Journal*
> *The Booklist* of the American Library
> Association
> *The Bulletin of the Center for Children's Books*,
> published by the University of Illinois at Urbana
> *Horn Book*
> *Kirkus Reviews*

As they pursue their careers in children's books, many authors subscribe to one or more of these periodicals as a way to keep up with what's going on in the field. *Horn Book* is the most "literary" of the publications, with articles in each issue by authors, illustrators, and critics, as well as reviews of recommended current books, while *School Library Journal*, which prints unfavorable reviews along with favorable notices, offers the most comprehensive review coverage.

When their books are published, many new authors feel they should do something on their own to help promote them. Some dream of being interviewed on national television, others have the more realistic expectation of an autograph signing at a local bookstore. Such publicity efforts boost an author's ego, but they don't usually generate many sales—especially of a first book. Far more crucial to the success of any children's book are favorable reviews in the five periodicals mentioned above, followed up by other recommendations and purchases by school and public libraries across the country. The latter are generated by the 400-plus review copies of each new juvenile title that the publisher sends out to major library systems, such as the Los Angeles County Board of Education; the Public Library of Atlanta, Georgia; and the State Department of Education in Augusta, Maine.

These promotional mailings are bolstered, of course, by the efforts of the publisher's sales reps to get a good selection of each season's books into bookstores everywhere. But authors, illustrators, and editors have to accept a basic reality of the business: Most bookstores, even specialty children's bookshops, devote the bulk of their shelf space to colorfully illustrated picture and gift books and paperback reprints, and have room for only a relatively small number of hardcover fiction and nonfiction titles. A few of the picture books and novels take off in a major way and become best-sellers in bookstores, but many sell slowly and eventually go back to their publishers in the form of returns.

Meanwhile, the library market is far more consistent, despite frequent budget cuts. If a book receives good reviews in the library media, it's likely to enjoy a solid sale—and there are almost no returns in the library market, save for damaged copies. So don't be surprised, or unduly disappointed, if you don't find your book in bookstores. Check instead at your local library, and chances are you'll find it on the shelves or in the computerized catalogue.

Both new and well-known authors often ask me how long they can expect to see their books remain in print. That's an almost impossible question to answer in a general way. A few books quickly establish themselves as outstanding examples of their kind and stay in print for decades. But most books have a much shorter life span. If they receive good reviews in the library media, they'll probably enjoy solid sales for several years, and then experience a dropoff, more drastic in some cases than others. Then it's up to the individual publisher to decide whether he can afford to keep the book going with a small reprint, or whether, however reluctantly, he'll have to let it go out of print. It's probably safe to say that most hard cover children's books stay in print for at least two to three years, and many titles rack up life spans of six to eight years or more.

## The second time around

In the meantime, one hopes the authors have gone on to write and publish other books. For many authors, the second book is the hardest. They're afraid they won't be able to recapture whatever it was that made the first book a success. The one bit of advice I give authors in this dilemma is to relax, forget there was a previous book, and treat the second book as if it were the first. For the truth is that every new book you write is in some way a first book, no matter how many titles you may have to your credit.

As your career develops, there are several pitfalls you should do your best to avoid. If you are still trying to place your first book, you may find it hard to believe, but there could come a time—if you are prolific—when you'll find yourself signing contracts with three or more different publishers. There's nothing intrinsically wrong with this; however, you may one day feel that you've spread yourself too thin.

On the other hand, in the existing publishing climate, you shouldn't rely too heavily on anyone house or editor, either. Back in the 1950s and 1960s, independent publishers abounded and once a children's book editor became the head of a department, he or she tended to stay in the job until retirement. That's no longer the case. Currently, mergers and acquisitions are commonplace in publishing, and children's book editors seem to be in constant motion.

This editorial flux has had a devastating effect on

authors, both beginning and well-established. Sometimes a new author has rejoiced when an editor has bought his first book, only to learn a few months later that that editor has left, and his or her replacement has no interest in the book and wants to cancel the contract. Or an established author who's published a string of successful novels with a particular editor is shocked when his successor declines the author's latest effort with a terse letter that's little more than a form rejection.

As authors attempt to steer their way through the treacherous undercurrents of today's publishing scene, they may fall victim to depression and despair. It's easy to lose your confidence when acceptance suddenly turns to rejection. If that occurs, the only thing to do is try to maintain your sense of perspective while you assess where you are as a writer, and plot a new course of action.

Sometimes this may mean, to paraphrase the old song, "picking yourself up, dusting yourself off, and starting all over again." If it does, you should hold to the writing standards you've developed over the years, remember your past successes as well as your failures, and send out query letters about your latest book to a new list of editors. If you project a positive attitude, it's likely editors will respond in kind, and you'll soon regain your confidence.

## A lasting impact

Despite all the vagaries of publishing today, it's still possible to build and sustain a satisfying career in the children's book field. So, whether you're just starting out or are well on your way, take heart. Writing books for children and young people has never been easy, but few other fields of writing are as rewarding. For, unlike many of their adult counterparts, children's books can have a unique and lasting impact on their impressionable young readers. I still remember poring over the illustrations and savoring the words of Wanda Gag's

*Millions of Cats*, Robert Lawson's and Munro Leaf's *The Story of Ferdinand*, and Marguerite de Angeli's *Skippack School*; I'm sure you have equally vivid memories of your own childhood favorites.

Not that every children's book that's published assumes the dimensions of a classic; far from it. But who knows? The picture book, nonfiction work, or novel that you're working on today may be enjoyed by thousands of young readers in a few years' time, and still be alive in their memories 50 years from now. Consciously or unconsciously, that's one of the goals most children's writers aim for—and many achieve it. I hope you will, too.

# Suggested Reading

## Awards

### Newbery Medal Winners

**2010 Winner**
Stead, Rebecca. *When You Reach Me.* New York: Wendy Lamb Books, 2009.

**2009 Winner**
Gaiman, Neil. *The Graveyard Book.* New York: HarperCollins, 2008.

**2008 Winner**
Schlitz, Laura Amy. *Good Masters! Sweet Ladies! Voices from a Medieval Village.* Somerville, MA: Candlewick Press, 2007.

### Caldecott Medal

**2010 Winner**
Pinkney, Jerry. *The Lion & the Mouse.* New York: Little, Brown, 2009.

**2009 Winner**
Swanson, Susan Marie (au) and Krommes, Beth (illus). *The House in the Night.* New York: Houghton Mifflin, 2008.

**2008 Winner**
Selznick, Brian. *The Invention of Hugo Cabret.* New York: Scholastic Press, 2007.

### *Boston Globe-Horn Book* **Awards**

**2010 Winner – Fiction and Poetry**
Stead, Rebecca. *When You Reach Me.* New York: Wendy Lamb Books, 2009.

**2010 Winner – Nonfiction**
Partridge, Elizabeth. *Marching for Freedom.* New York: Viking, 2009.

**2010 Winner – Picture Book**
Croza, Laurel. *I Know Here.* Toronto, ON: Groundwood, 2009.

**2009 Winner – Fiction and Poetry**
Pratchett, Terry. *Nation.* New York: HarperCollins, 2008.

**2009 Winner – Nonfiction**
Fleming, Candace. *The Lincolns: A Scrapbook Look at Abraham and Mary.* New York: Schwartz & Wade, 2008.

**2009 Winner – Picture Book**
Mahy, Margaret. *Bubble Trouble.* New York: Clarion, 2008.

**2008 Winner – Fiction and Poetry**
Alexie, Sherman. *The Absolutely True Diary of a Part-Time Indian.* New York: Little, Brown, 2007.

**2008 Winner – Nonfiction**
Sis, Peter. *The Wall.* New York: Farrar, Straus and Giroux, 2007.

**2008 Winner – Picture Book**
Bean, Jonathan. *At Night.* New York: Farrar, Straus and Giroux, 2007.


**Jane Addams**
**2010 Winner – Books for Younger Children**
Winter, Jeanette. *Nasreen's Secret School: A True Story from Afghanistan.* New York: Beach Lane Books, 2009.

**2010 Winner – Books for Older Children**
Partridge, Elizabeth. *Marching for Freedom.* New York: Viking, 2009.

**2009 Winner – Books for Younger Children**
Nivola, Claire A. *Planting the Trees of Kenya.* New York: Frances Foster Books, 2008.

**2009 Winner – Books for Older Children**
Engle, Margarita. *The Surrender Tree.* New York: Henry Holt, 2008.

**2008 Winner – Books for Younger Children**
McCully, Emily Arnold. *The Escape of Oney Judge.* New York: Farrar, Straus and Giroux, 2007.

**2008 Winner – Books for Older Children**
Brimner, Larry Dane. *We Are One.* Honesdale, PA: Calkins Creek Books, 2007.

## Coretta Scott King Award

**2010 Winner**
Nelson, Vaunda Micheaux. *Bad News for Outlaws.* Minneapolis, MN: Carolrhoda Books, 2009.

**2009 Winner**
Nelson, Kadir. *We Are the Ship.* New York: Jump at the Sun, 2008.

**2008 Winner**
Curtis, Christopher Paul. *Elijah of Buxton.* New York: Scholastic, 2007.

## Michael L. Printz Award

**2010 Winner**
Bray, Libba. *Going Bovine.* New York: Delacorte, 2009.

**2009 Winner**
Marchetta, Melina. *Jellicoe Road.* New York: HarperTeen, 2008.

**2008 Winner**
McCaughrean, Geraldine. *The White Darkness.* New York: HarperTeen, 2007.

## Christopher Awards
## 2010

**Preschool Winner**
Heo, Yumi. *Ten Days and Nine Nights.* New York: Schwartz & Wade, 2009.

**Ages 6-8 Winner**
Dennis, Brian; Kirby Larson; and Mary Nethery. *Nubs: The True Story of a Mutt, a Marine, and a Miracle.* New York: Little, Brown, 2009.

**Ages 8-10 Winner**
Hegamin, Tonya Cherie. *Most Loved in All the World.* New York: Houghton Mifflin, 2008.

**Ages 10-12 Winner**
Clements, Andrew. *Extra Credit.* New York: Atheneum, 2009.

**Young Adult Winner**
McClure, Tori Murden. *A Pearl in the Storm*. New York: HarperCollins, 2009.

## 2009

**Preschool Winner**
Kajikawa, Kimiko. *Close to You*. New York: Henry Holt, 2008.

**Ages 6-8 Winner**
Henson, Heather. *That Book Woman*. New York: Atheneum, 2008.

**Ages 8-10 Winner**
Pennypacker, Sara. *Clementine's Letter*. New York: Disney-Hyperion, 2008.

**Ages 10-12 Winner**
Dowell, Frances O'Roark. *Shooting the Moon*. New York: Atheneum, 2008.

**Young Adult Winner**
Myers, Walter Dean. *Sunrise Over Fallujah*. New York: Scholastic Press, 2008.

## Golden Kite Awards
## 2010

**Fiction Winner**
Durango, Julia. *Sea of the Dead*. New York: S & S Books for Young Readers, 2009.

**Nonfiction Winner**
Bryan, Ashley. *Ashley Bryan: Words to My Life's Song*. New York: Atheneum, 2009.

**Picture Book Text Winner**
Bauer, Marion Dane. *The Longest Night*. New York: Holiday House, 2009.

**Picture Book Illustration Winner**
Mora, Pat (au) and John Parra (illus). *Gracias Thanks*. New York: Lee & Low Books, 2009.

## 2009

**Fiction Winner**

Watkins, Steve. *Down Sand Mountain*. Somerville, MA: Candlewick Press, 2008.

**Nonfiction Winner**

Turner, Pamela S. *A Life in the Wild*. New York: Farrar, Straus and Giroux, 2008.

**Picture Book Text Winner**

Becker, Bonny. *A Visitor for Bear*. Somerville, MA: Candlewick Press, 2008.

**Picture Book Illustration Winner**

Yum, Hyewon. *Last Night*. New York: Farrar, Straus and Giroux, 2008.

## 2008

**Fiction Winner**

Applegate, Katherine. *Home of the Brave*. New York: Feiwel and Friends, 2007.

**Nonfiction Winner**

Bausum, Ann. *Muckrakers*. Washington, DC: National Geographic, 2007.

**Picture Book Text Winner**

Pennypacker, Sara. *Pierre in Love*. New York: Orchard Books, 2007.

**Picture Book Illustration Winner**

Morales, Yuyi. *Little Night*. New York: Roaring Brook Press, 2007.

## Robert F. Sibert Awards

**2010 Medal Winner**

Stone, Tanya Lee. *Almost Astronauts: 13 Women Who Dared to Dream*. Somerville, MA: Candlewick Press, 2009.

**2009 Medal Winner**

Nelson, Kadir. *We Are the Ship*. New York: Jump at the Sun, 2008.

**2008 Medal Winner**

Sis, Peter. *The Wall*. New York: Farrar, Straus and Giroux, 2007.

## National Book Awards

**2009**

Hoose, Phillip. *Claudette Colvin: Twice Toward Justice.* New York: Farrar, Straus and Giroux, 2008.

**2008**

Blundell, Judy. *What I Saw and How I Lied.* New York: Scholastic, 2007.

## Scott O'Dell Award for Historical Fiction

**2010**

Phelan, Matt. *The Storm in the Barn.* Somerville, MA: Candlewick Press, 2009.

**2009**

Anderson, Laurie Halse. *Chains.* New York: Simon & Schuster, 2008.

**2008**

Curtis, Christopher Paul. *Elijah of Buxton.* New York: Scholastic, 2007.

## Orbis Pictus Awards

**2010**

Bass, Hester. *The Secret World of Walter Anderson.* Somerville, MA: Candlewick Press, 2009.

**2009**

Tanaka, Shelley. *Amelia Earhart.* New York: Abrams Books for Young Readers, 2008.

**2008**

Bolden, Tonya. *MLK: Journey of a King.* New York: Abrams Books for Young Readers, 2007.

## International Reading Association Awards
### 2010

**Primary – Fiction**

Scanlon, Liz Garton. *All the World.* New York: Beach Lane Books, 2009.

**Primary – Nonfiction**

Rodriguez, Rachel. *Building on Nature.* New York: Henry Holt, 2009.

**Intermediate – Fiction**
Houts, Michelle. *The Beef Princess of Practical County.* New York: Delacorte, 2009.

**Intermediate – Fiction**
Kelly, Jacqueline. *The Evolution of Calpurnia Tate.* New York: Henry Holt, 2009.

**Young Adult – Fiction**
Stead, Rebecca. *When You Reach Me.* New York: Wendy Lamb Books, 2009.

## 2009

**Primary – Fiction**
Randall, Alison L. *The Wheat Doll.* Atlanta, GA: Peachtree, 2008.

**Primary – Nonfiction**
Berne, Jennifer. *Manfish.* San Francisco, CA: Chronicle, 2008.

**Intermediate – Fiction**
Nuzum, K. A. *The Leanin' Dog.* New York: HarperCollins, 2008.

**Intermediate – Nonfiction**
Beccia, Carlyn. *The Raucous Royals.* Boston, MA: Houghton Mifflin, 2008.

**Young Adult – Fiction**
Ayarbe, Heidi. *Freeze Frame.* New York: HarperCollins, 2008.

**Young Adult – Nonfiction**
Li, Moying. *Snow Falling in Spring.* New York: Farrar, Straus and Giroux, 2008.

# Picture Books for Youngest Readers

## Board Books

Apperley, Dawn. *Dad Mine!* New York: Little, Brown, 2003.
Barton, Byron. *My Car.* New York: Greenwillow, 2001.
Emberley, Rebecca. *My Colors/Mia Colores.* New York: Little, Brown, 2000.
Henkes, Kevin. *Owen's Marshmallow Chick.* New York: Harper Festival, 2002.
Hines, Anna Grossnickle. *What Can You Do in the Sun?* New York: Greenwillow, 1999.

Inkpen, Mick. *Wibbly Pig Likes Bananas.* New York: Viking, 1995.
Lionni, Leon. *Let's Play.* Knopf, 2003.
Manning, Jane. *My First Baby Games.* New York: HarperFestival, 2001.
Marzollo, Jean. *Papa Papa.* New York: HarperFestival, 2000.
Suen, Anastasia. *Toddler Two.* New York: Lee & Low, 2000.
Weninger, Brigitte. *A Child Is a Child.* New York: Penguin, 2004.
Yaccarino, Dan. *Good Night, Mr. Night.* New York: Harcourt, 1997.
Yee, Wong Herbert. *Here Come Trainmice!* New York: Houghton, 2000.

### Wordless Picturebooks

Alborough, Jez. *Hug.* Cambridge, MA: Candlewick, 2002.
Baker, Jeannie. *Home.* New York: Greenwillow, 2004.
Briggs, Raymond. *The Snowman.* New York: Random, 2000.
DePaola, Tomie. *Pancakes for Breakfast.* New York: Harcourt, 1978.
Meyer, Mercer. *A Boy, A Dog, and a Frog.* New York: Dial, 1967.
Rogers, Gregory. *The Boy, The Bear, The Baron, The Bard.* Brookfield, CT:
    Roaring Brook, 2004.
Tafuri, Nancy. *Have You Seen My Duckling?* New York: Tipelo, 1996.
Ward, Lynd. *The Silver Pony.* Boston: Houghton, 1973.
Wiesner, David. *Sector 7.* New York: Clarion, 1999.

### Picture Books in Verse

Brenner, Barbara. *Good Morning, Garden.* Chanhassen, MN: Northwood,
    2004.
Charlip, Remy. *Sleepytime Rhyme.* New York: Greenwillow, 1991.
Curtis, Jamie and Cornell, Laura. *It's Hard to Be Five: Learning How to
    Work My Control Panel.* New York: HarperCollins, 2004.
Davis, Jill. *My Busy Day.* New York: Viking, 2004.
Hesse, Karen. *The Cats in Krasinski Square.* New York: Scholastic, 2004.
Ho, Minfong. *Peek! A Thai Hide-And-Seek.* Cambridge, MA: Candlewick,
    2004.
Hunter, Ryan Ann. *Robots Slither.* New York: Putnam, 2004.
Kirk, Daniel. *Snow Dude.* New York: Hyperion, 2002.
O'Garden, Irene. *The Scrubbly-Bubbly Car Wash.* New York:
    HarperCollins, 2003.
Rosenthal, Betsy R. *My House Is Singing.* New York: Harcourt, 2004.
Ryan, Pam Muñoz. *Mud Is Cake.* New York: Hyperion, 2002.

## Concept and Novelty books

Alder, David A. *How Tall, How Short, How Faraway?* New York: Holiday, 1999.

Beil, Karen Magnuson. *Mooove Over! About Counting by Twos.* New York: Holiday, 2004.

Chitwood, Suzanne Tanner. *Wake Up, Big Barn.* New York: Scholastic, 2002.

Cotton, Cynthia. *At the Edge of the Woods: A Counting Book.* New York: Holt, 2002.

Freyman, Saxton and Elffers, Joost. *Food for Thought: The Complete Book of Concepts for Growing Minds.* New York: Arthur A. Levine, 2005.

Gray, Kes. *Cluck O'Clock.* New York: Holiday, 2004.

Greene, Rhonda Gowler. *When a Line Bends . . . a Shape Begins.* New York: Houghton, 1997.

Hills, Tad. *My Fuzzy Friends.* New York: Little Simon, 1999.

Howell, Will. *Zooflakes ABC.* New York: Walker, 2002.

Lester, Mike. *A Is for Salad.* New York: Putnam, 2002.

Markes, Julie. *Shhhh! Everybody's Sleeping.* New York: HarperCollins, 2005.

Packard, Edward. *Big Numbers and Pictures That Show Just How Big They Are.* Brookfield, CT: Millbrook, 2000

Pinczes, Elinor J. *Inchworm and a Half.* New York: Houghton, 2001.

Schwartz, David M. *G Is for Googol: A Math Alphabet Book.* Berkeley, CA: Tricycle, 2000.

Wormell, Christopher. *Teeth, Tails, and Tentacles: An Animal Counting Book.* Philadelphia: Running Press, 2004.

# Picture Story Books

Christelow, Eileen. *Where's the Big Bad Wolf?* New York: Clarion, 2002.

Clement, Rod. *Grandpa's Teeth.* New York: HarperCollins, 1998.

Ernst, Lisa Campbell. *Stella Louella's Runaway Book.* New York: Simon & Schuster, 1998.

Feiffer, Jules. *Bark, George.* New York: HarperCollins, 1999.

Fleischman, Paul. *Sidewalk Circus.* Cambridge, MA: Candlewick, 2004.

Henkes, Kevin. *So Happy!* New York: Greenwillow, 2005.

Hurd, Thacher. *Art Dog.* New York: HarperCollins, 1996.

Kellogg, Steven. *The Missing Mitten Mystery.* New York: Puffin, 2000.

Kimmel, Eric A. *Cactus Soup.* Tarrytown, NY: Marshall Cavendish, 2004.

Kopelke, Lisa. *Tissue, Please!* New York: Simon & Schuster, 2004.

Krosoczka, Jarrett J. *Baghead.* Knopf, 2002.

Krupinski, Loretta. *The Royal Mice: The Sword and the Horn.* New York: Hyperion, 2004.
Laden, Nina. *The Night I Followed the Dog.* New York: Chronicle, 1994.
Lass, Bonnie, and Sturges, Philemon. *Who Took the Cookies from the Cookie Jar?* New York: Little, Brown, 2000.
Levy, Constance. *The Story of Red Rubber Ball.* New York: Harcourt, 2004.
McClements, George. *Jake Gander, Storyville Detective.* New York: Hyperion, 2002.
Myers, Tim. *Basho and the River Stones.* New York: Marshall Cavendish, 2004.
Palatini, Margie. *The Web Files.* New York: Hyperion, 2001.
Pearson, Tracey Campbell. *Where Does Joe Go?* New York: Farrar, 1999.
Samuels, Barbara. *Dolores on Her Toes.* New York: Farrar, 2003.
Smith, Will. *Just the Two of Us.* New York: Scholastic, 2001.
Walsh, Ellen Stoll. *Dot and Jabber and the Great Acorn Mystery.* New York: Harcourt, 2001.
Willey, Margaret. *Clever Beatrice and the Best Little Pony.* New York: Atheneum, 2004.
Wise, William. *Christopher Mouse: The Tale of a Small Traveler.* New York: Bloomsbury, 2004.
Wisniewski, David. *Tough Cookie.* New York: HarperCollins, 1999.

## Mood Picture Books

Bang, Molly. *One Fall Day.* New York: Greenwillow, 1994.
Banks, Kate. *And If the Moon Could Talk.* Frances Foster Books, 2004.
Bradman, Tony. *Daddy's Lullaby.* New York: Margaret K. McElderry, 2001.
Burleigh, Robert. *Lookin' for Bird in the Big City.* New York: HarperCollins, 2001.
Daniels, Teri. *Just Enough.* New York: Viking, 2000.
Keller, Holly. *Pearl's New Skates.* New York: Greenwillow, 2005.
London, Jonathan. *Sun Dance, Water Dance.* New York: Dutton, 2001.
Moss, Miriam. *Don't Forget I Love You.* New York: Dial, 2004.
Taylor, Debbie A. *Sweet Music in Harlem.* New York: Lee and Low, 2004.

## Multicultural Picture Books

English, Karen. *Hot Day on Abbott Avenue.* New York: Clarion, 2004.
Gunning, Monica. *A Shelter in Our Car.* San Francisco: Children's Book Press, 2004.

Harrington, Janice N. *Going North.* New York: Farrar, 2004.
Hesse, Karen. *Come on, Rain!* New York: Scholastic, 1999.
Hooks, Bell. *Skin Again.* New York: Hyperion, 2004.
Roberts, Brenda C. *Jazzy Miz Mozetta.* New York: Farrar, 2004.

## Nonfiction Picture Books

Aliki. *Ah, Music!* New York: HarperCollins, 2003.
Bang, Molly. *My Light.* New York: Scholastic/Blue Sky, 2004.
Banks, Kate. *A Gift from the Sea.* New York: Frances Foster Books (Farrar), 2001.
Banks, Kate. *The Night Worker.* New York: Frances Foster Books (Farrar), 2000.
Berger, Melvin and Berger, Gilda. *Penguins Swim but Don't Get Wet and Other Amazing Facts about Polar Animals.* New York: Scholastic, 2004.
Carle, Eric. *Mister Seahorse.* New York: Philomel, 2004.
Cherry, Lynne. *The Sea, the Storm and the Mangrove Tangle.* New York: Farrar, 2004.
Christelow, Eileen. *Vote!* New York: Clarion, 2003.
Jenkins, Steve. *Actual Size.* New York: Houghton, 2004.
Lorenz, Albert. *Journey to Cahokia.* New York: Abrams, 2003.
Lyon, George Ella. *Weaving the Rainbow.* New York: Atheneum, 2004.
Rinck, Maranke. *The Prince Child.* Asheville, NC and Rotterdam: Front Street/Liminiscaat, 2004.
Rockwell, Anne. *Our Earth.* New York: Harcourt, 1998.
Sis, Peter. *The Train of States.* New York: Greenwillow, 2004.
Smith, David J. *If the World Were a Village.* Kids Can, 2002.
Staake, Bob. *Hello, Robots.* New York: Viking, 2004.
Thompson, Lauren. *Polar Bear at Night.* New York: Scholastic, 2004.
Wallace, Karen. *I Am a Tyrannosaurus.* New York: Atheneum, 2004.
Weatherby, Brenda and Weatherby, Mark. *The Trucker.* New York: Scholastic, 2004.
Winnick, Karen B. *The Night of the Fireflies.* Honesdale, PA: Boyds Mills, 2004.

## Picture Book Biography

Adler, David A. *A Picture Book of Louis Braille.* New York: Holiday, 1997.
Atkins, Jeannine. *Mary Anning and the Sea Dragon.* New York: Farrar, 1999.
Bartoletti, Susan Campbell. *The Flag Maker.* New York: Houghton, 2004.

Burleigh, Robert. *Amelia Earhart Free in the Skies.* New York: Harcourt, 2003.

Burleigh, Robert. *Into the Air: The Story of the Wright Brothers' First Flight.* New York: Harcourt, 2002.

Cline-Ransome, Lesa. *Major Taylor: Champion Cyclist.* New York: Atheneum, 2004.

Davies, Jacqueline. *The Boy Who Drew Birds: A Story of John James Audubon.* Boston: Houghton Mifflin, 2004.

Demi. *Muhammad.* New York: Simon & Schuster, 2003.

Dunlap, Julie and Lorbiecki, Marybeth. *John Muir and Stickeen: An Icy Adventure with a No-Good Dog.* Chanhassen, MN: Northwood, 2004.

Gantos, Jack. *Hole in My Life.* New York: Farrar, 2002.

Greenberg, Jan and Jordan, Sandra. *Action Jackson.* Brookfield, CT: Roaring Brook Press/The Millbrook Press, 2002.

Jacobson, Rick. *Picasso: Soul on Fire.* Toronto: Tundra, 2004.

Kerley, Barbara. *Walt Whitman: Words for America.* New York: Scholastic, 2004.

McCully, Emily Arnold. *Squirrel and John Muir.* New York: Farrar, 2004.

Myers, Walter Dean. *I've Seen the Promised Land: The Life of Martin Luther King, Jr.* New York: HarperCollins, 2004.

Rappaport, Doreen. *John's Secret Dreams: The Life of John Lennon.* New York: Hyperion, 2004.

Ryan, Pam Muñoz. *Amelia and Eleanor Go for a Ride: Based on a True Story.* New York: Scholastic, 2000.

Ryan, Pam Muñoz. *When Marian Sang* (Illustrated by Brian Selznick). New York: Scholastic, 2002.

Shange, Ntozake. *Ellington Was Not a Street.* New York: Simon & Schuster, 1983.

Warren, Andrea. *Escape from Saigon: How a Vietnam War Orphan Became an American Boy.* New York: Farrar, 2004.

# Easy Readers

Blume, Judy. *The One in the Middle Is the Green Kangaroo.* Scarsdale, New York: Bradbury, 1981.

Calhoun, Mary. *Cross-Country Cat.* New York: Morrow, 1986.

Calhoun, Mary. *Hot-Air Henry.* New York: Mulberry, 1986.

Clements, Andrew. *Tara and Tiree, Fearless Friends.* New York: Simon & Schuster, 2002.

Corey, Shana. *First Graders from Mars.* New York: Scholastic, 2001.

dePaola, Tomie. *The Art Lesson.* New York: Putnam, 1989.

Hutchins, Pat. *The Very Worst Monster.* New York: Greenwillow, 1985.
Kraus, Robert. *Where Are You Going Little Mouse?* New York: Greenwillow, 1986.
Sharmat, Marjorie Weinman. *Nate the Great.* New York: Bantam, 1972.
Van Leeuwen, Jean. *More Tales of Oliver Pig.* New York: Puffin, 1993.

# Chapter Books

## Series

Adler, David A. Cam Jensen. New York: Viking.
Adler, David A. The Bones Series. New York: Viking.
Brown, Marc. Arthur. New York: Little, Brown.
Conford, Ellen. Annabel the Actress. New York: Simon & Schuster.
Danziger, Paula. Amber Brown. New York: Scholastic.
Hale, Bruce. Chet Gecko–Private Eye. Orlando, FL: Harcourt.
Osborne, Mary Pope. Magic Tree House. New York: Random.
Park, Barbara. Junie B. Jones. New York: Random.
Roy, Ron. A to Z Mysteries. New York: Random.
Sachar, Louis. Marvin Redpost. New York: Random.
Wojciechowski, Susan. Beany. Cambridge, MA: Candlewick.

## Separate Titles

Auch, Mary Jane. *I Was a Third Grade Science Project.* New York: Holiday, 1998.
Buchanan, Jane. *The Berry-Picking Man.* New York: Farrar, 2003.
Clements, Andrew. *Jake Drake, Class Clown.* New York: Simon & Schuster, 2002.
dePaola, Tomie. *26 Fairmont Avenue.* New York: Putnam, 1999.
Duffey, Betsy. *Cody Unplugged.* New York: Viking, 1999.
Freeman, Martha. *The Trouble with Cats.* New York: Holiday, 2000.
Freschet, Gina. *Up and at 'Em with Winny & Ernst.* New York: Farrar, 2005.
Graves, Bonnie. *Taking Care of Trouble.* New York: Dutton, 2002.
Green, Stephanie. *Owen Foote, Super Spy.* New York: Clarion, 2001.
Haddix, Margaret Peterson. *The Girl with 500 Middle Names.* New York: Simon & Schuster, 2001.
King-Smith, Dick. *Lady Lollipopu.* Cambridge, MA: Candlewick, 2001.
Kline, Suzy. *Herbie Jones Moves On.* New York: Putnam, 2003.
Lowry, Lois. *Gooney Bird Greene.* New York: Houghton, 2002.
McDonald, Megan. *Judy Moody Gets Famous!* Cambridge, MA: Candlewick, 2001.

Morgenstern, Susie. *A Book of Coupons*. New York: Viking, 2001.

Nagda, Ann Whitehead. *Dear Whiskers*. New York: Holiday, 2000.

Rylant, Cynthia. *Mr. Putter & Tabby Write the Book*. New York: Harcourt, 2004.

Seuling, Barbara. *Oh, No, It's Robert*. Chicago: Cricket, 1999.

## Myth, Legend, Nursery and Folktales

Fox, Frank G. *Jean Laffite and the Big Ol' Whale*. New York: Farrar, 2003.

Hamilton, Virginia. *The People Could Fly: The Picture Book*. New York: Knopf, 2004.

Hodges, Margaret. *Merlin and the Making of the King*. New York: Holiday, 2004.

Kellogg, Stephen. *Mike Fink*. New York: Farrar, 2003.

Kellogg, Stephen. *Sally Ann Thunder Ann Whirlwind Crockett*. New York: HarperCollins, 1995.

Lester, Julius. *John Henry*. New York: Dial, 1994.

McCaughrean, Geraldine. *Odysseus*. Chicago: Cricket, 2004.

McDermott, Gerald. *Jabuti the Tortoise: A Trickster Tale*. New York: Harcourt, 2001.

Reneaux, J. J. *Cajun Folktales*. Little Rock: August House, 1992.

Salley, Coleen. *Who's That Tripping over My Bridge?* Gretna, LA: Pelican, 2002.

Schanzer, Rosalyn. *Davy Crockett Saves the World*. New York: HarperCollins, 2001.

Stanley, Diane. *The Giant and the Beanstalk*. New York: HarperCollins, 2004.

Trivizas, Eugene. *The Three Little Wolves and the Big Bad Pig*. New York: Simon & Schuster, 1993.

Wisniewski, David. *Golem*. New York: Clarion, 1996.

## Middle Grade (Ages 8 – 12)

### Historical Fiction

Curtis, Christopher Paul. *Bud, Not Buddy*. New York: Delacourt, 1999.

Curtis, Christopher Paul. *The Watsons Go to Birmingham—1963*. New York: Bantam, 1997.

Cushman, Karen. *Rodzina*. New York: Clarion, 2003.

Divakaruni, Chitra Banerjee. *The Conch Bearer*. Brookfield, CT: Roaring Brook, 2003.

Fox, Paula. *The Slave Dancer*. New York: Dell, 1991.
Giff, Patricia Reilly. *Lily's Crossing*. New York: Bantam, 1999.
Giff, Patricia Reilly. *Nory Ryan's Song*. New York: Delacorte, 2000.
Hale, Marian. *The Truth about Sparrows*. New York: Holt, 2004.
Hesse, Karen. *Out of the Dust*. New York: Scholastic, 1997.
Hesse, Karen. *Stowaway*. New York: McElderry, 2000.
Hesse, Karen. *Witness*. New York: Scholastic, 2001.
Hobbs, Will. *Down the Yukon*. New York: HarperCollins, 2001.
Osborne, Mary Pope. *Adaline Falling Star*. New York: Scholastic, 2000.
Peck, Richard. *A Long Way from Chicago*. New York: Dial, 1998.
Peck, Richard. *The Teacher's Funeral: A Comedy in Three Parts*. New York: Dial, 2004.
Schmidt, Gary D. *Lizzie Bright and the Buckminster Boy*. New York: Clarion, 2004.
Taylor, Mildred D. *Roll of Thunder, Hear My Cry*. New York: Phyllis Fogelman, 2001.
Wolff, Virginia Euwer. *Make Lemonade*. New York: Holt, 1993.
Woodson, Jacqueline. *Locomotion*. New York: Putnam, 2003.

### Multicultural

Crutcher, Chris. *Whale Talk*. New York: Laurel Leaf, 2001.
Curtis, Christopher Paul. *Bucking the Sarge*. Random/Wendy Lamb, 2004.
Ellis, Deborah. *Breadwinner*. Toronto: Douglas & McIntire, 2001.
Joseph, Lynn. *The Color of My Words*. New York: HarperCollins, 2000.
Myers, Walter Dean. *Handbook for Boys*. New York: HarperCollins, 2002.
Na, An. *A Step from Heaven*. Asheville, NC: Front Street, 2001.
Ryan, Pam Muñoz. *Esperanza Rising*. New York: Scholastic, 2000.
Spinelli, Jerry. *Maniac Magee*. New York: Scholastic, 1990.
Whelan, Gloria. *Homeless Bird*. New York: HarperCollins, 2000.
Woodson, Jacqueline. *From the Notebooks of Melanin Sun*. New York: Scholastic/Blue Sky, 1995.

### Fantasy and Science Fiction

Alexander, Lloyd. *The Book of Three*. New York: Holt, 1999.
Babbitt, Natalie. *Tuck Everlasting*. New York: Farrar, 1975.
Colfer, Eoin. *Artemis Fowl*. New York: Hyperion, 1991.
Constable, Kate. *The Singer of All Songs*. New York: Scholastic, 2004.
Cooper, Susan. *Over Sea, Under Stone*. San Diego: Harcourt, 1993.
Coville, Bruce. *Jeremy Thatcher, Dragon Hatcher*. New York: Pocket Books, 1991.

Haddix, Margaret Peterson. *Running Out of Time.* New York: Simon & Schuster, 1995.
Hesse, Karen. *Music of Dolphins.* New York: Scholastic, 1996.
L'Engle, Madeleine. *A Wrinkle in Time.* New York: Ariel, 1962.
Lowry, Lois. *The Giver.* New York: Doubleday, 1993.
Rowling, J. K. *Harry Potter and the Chamber of Secrets.* New York: Scholastic, 2002.
Sachar, Louis. *Holes.* New York: Farrar, 1998.
Snicket, Lemony. *A Series of Unfortunate Events.* New York: HarperCollins, 2002.

## Animal Fantasies

Cleary, Beverly. *The Mouse and the Motorcycle.* New York: HarperCollins, 1965.
Howe, James. *Howliday Inn.* New York: Avon, 1982.
Jacques, Brian. *Rakkety Tam.* New York: Philomel, 2004.
Jacques, Brian. *Redwall.* New York: Ace, 1998.
Smith, Dodie. *101 Dalmatians.* New York: Avon, 1982.
White, E. B. *Charlotte's Web.* HarperCollins, 1980.
White, E. B. *Stuart Little.* New York: HarperTrophy, 1972.
Wise, William. *Christopher Mouse: The Tale of a Small Traveler.* New York: Bloomsbury, 2004.

## Realistic Novels

Auch, Mary Jane. *I Was a Third Grade Science Project.* New York: Holiday, 1998.
Avi and Rachel Vail. *Nevermind! A Twin Novel.* New York: HarperCollins, 2004.
Blume, Judy. *Blubber.* New York: Atheneum, 2001.
Cameron, Ann. *The Stories Huey Tells.* New York: Yearling, 1995.
Cleary, Beverly. *Beezus and Ramona.* New York: Avon, 1990.
Clements, Andrew. *Frindle.* New York: Aladdin, 1998.
Creech, Sharon. *Chasing Redbird.* New York: HarperTrophy, 1998.
DiCamillo, Kate. *Because of Winn-Dixie.* Cambridge, MA: Candlewick, 2000.
Fenner, Carol. *The King of Dragons.* New York: Simon & Schuster, 1998.
Fitzhugh, Louise. *Harriet the Spy.* New York: Dell Yearling, 2001.
Gantos, Jack. *Joey Pigza Swallowed the Key.* New York: Farrar, 1998.
Hiaasen, Carl. *Hoot.* New York: Knopf, 2002.
Myers, Walter Dean. *Darnell Rock Reporting.* New York: Yearling, 1994.

Paulsen, Gary. *Hatchet*. New York: Simon Pulse, 1999.
Philbrick, Rodman. *Freak the Mighty*. New York: Scholastic, 1993.
White, Ruth. *Belle Prater's Boy*. New York: Bantam, 1996.

## YA Novels (14 and Up)

Anderson, Laurie Halse. *Speak*. New York: Puffin, 2001.
Brashares, Ann. *The Sisterhood Of The Traveling Pants*. New York:
Laurel-Leaf, 2001.
Byars, Betsy. *The Pinballs*. New York: Harper, 1977.
Cabot, Meg. *All-American Girl*. New York: HarperCollins, 2002.
Cabot, Meg. *The Princess Diaries*.New York: HarperTrophy, 2001.
Cormier, Robert. *The Chocolate War*. New York: Panteon, 1974.
Flinn, Alex. *Breathing Underwater*. New York: HarperCollins, 2001.
Golding, William. *Lord of the Flies*. New York: Berkley, 2003.
Hinton, S. E. *The Outsiders*. New York: Puffin, 1997.
McCormick, Patricia. *Cut*. Asheville, NC: Front Street, 2000.
Willis-Holt, Kimberly. *My Louisiana Sky*. New York: Holt, 1998.

## Graphic Novels (All Ages)

Crilley, Mark. *Akiko v. 1 (The Menace of Alia Rellapor, Book One)*. Sirius,
1997.
Dezago, Todd. *Tellos: Reluctant Heroes*. Image Comics, 2001.
Eisner, Will. *The Last Knight: An Introduction to Don Quixote*. NBM, 2001.
Eisner, Will. *Moby Dick*. NBM, 2003.
Fisher, Jane Smith. *WJHC on the Air!* Wilson Place, 2003.
Gownley, Jimmy. *Amelia Rules! The Whole World's Crazy*. IBooks, 2003.
Huddleston, Courtney. *Decoy*. Penny Farthing, 2000.
Kunkel, Mike. *Herobear and the Kid: The Inheritance*. Astonish Comics,
2003.
Neubecker, Robert. *Wow! City!* New York: Hyperion, 2004.
O'Connor, George. *Kapow!* New York: Simon & Schuster, 2004.
Pickney, Brian. *Sparrowboy*. New York: Aladdin, 1997.
Prado, Miguelanxo. *Peter and the Wolf*. NBM, 2003.
Robinson, James. *Leave It to Chance: Shaman's Rain*. Image Comics,
1999.
Slott, Daniel. *Justice League Adventures*. DC Comics, 2003.
Smith, Jeff. *Bone: Out from Bonneville*. Cartoon Books, 2003.
Spiegelman, Art and Mouly, Francoise (eds.) *It Was a Dark and Silly Night*.
New York: HarperCollins, 2003.

# Nonfiction
## Nonfiction for Older Readers

Blacklock, Dyan. *The Roman Army: The Legendary Soldiers Who Created an Empire.* New York: Walker, 2004.

Davis, Kenneth C. *Don't Know Much About Planet Earth.* New York: HarperCollins, 2001.

Davis, Kenneth C. *Don't Know Much About American History.* New York: HarperCollins, 2003.

Dyson, Marianne J. *Home on the Moon: Living on a Space Frontier.* Washington D. C.: National Geographic, 2003.

Giblin, James Cross. *Secrets of the Sphinx.* New York: Scholastic, 2004.

Heller, Lora. *Sign Language for Kids: A Fun and Easy Guide to American Sign Language.* New York: Sterling, 2004.

McWhorter, Diane. *A Dream of Freedom: The Civil Rights Movement from 1954 to 1968.* New York: Scholastic, 2004.

## Biographies

Bloom Fradin, Judith & Dennis Fradin. *The Power of One: Daisy Bates and the Little Rock Nine.* New York: Clarion, 2004.

Bredeson, Carmen. *After the Last Dog Died: The True-Life, Hair-Raising Adventure of Douglas Mawson and His 1911-1914 Antarctic Expedition.* Washington, D. C.: National Geographic, 2003.

Cooper, Ilene. *Jack: The Early Years of John F. Kennedy.* New York: Dutton, 2003.

Mitchell, Elizabeth. *Journey to the Bottomless Pit. The Story of Stephen Bishop and Mammoth Cave.* New York: Viking, 2004.

*Barbara Stretton, who compiled this Suggested Reading list, was a teacher/librarian in elementary, junior high, and high schools for 28 years in Utah and Connecticut. She is the author of three fiction novels for young adults and two nonfiction books and is an Instructor with the Institute of Children's Literature. She also writes educational video scripts and study guides, including teachers' guides for Listening Library, the children's audiobook division of Random House.*

# Index